Called to Discipleship

TURNING TO
CHRIST
WITH FULL PURPOSE
OF HEART

Called to Discipleship

TURNING TO
CHRIST
WITH FULL PURPOSE
OF HEART

MICHAEL STEVEN PURLES

ARPress
ILLUMINATING IDEAS,
EMPOWERING VOICES

ARPress
45 Dan Road Suite 15
Canton, MA 02021

Hotline: 1(888) 821-0229
Fax: 1(508) 545-7580

Ordering Information:
Quantity sales. Special discounts are available on quantity purchases by corporations, associations, and others. For details, contact the publisher at the address above.

Printed in the United States of America.

ISBN-13:   Softcover   979-8-89676-092-4
                    eBook   979-8-89676-094-8
                    Hardback   979-8-89676-093-1

Library of Congress Control Number: 2025915347

TABLE OF CONTENTS

DEDICATION

———◆◇◆———

For Jerry, my wife of 55 years-

you are the love of my life and I am

incomplete without you.

AUTHOR'S NOTE

❧⊶⊙⟋⟍⊙⊷❧

One Sabbath (Sunday) morning, I was sitting in my home office, just gazing out the window as a beautiful summer day was slowly marching on. On the other side of the window, a red maple tree fills much of the available visual space. Its leaves seem to invite close inspection, the red color captivating.

As I was pondering on the beauty of this gift of nature, a hummingbird suddenly came into view. I was surprised to see it circling the tree looking for flowers, for nectar, I am sure. It was a joy watching the bird fly and then hover and then fly again, around and around the tree. Disappointment. No matter how hard it looked, no flowers were there to fulfill its quest, nor ever will be.

I couldn't help pondering on this interesting scene, as the intense desire of the bird and its efforts, no matter how sincere, could not make a maple tree sprout flowers. A comparison of this act in nature with that of our mortal lives provided a visual comparison regarding Heavenly Father's children striving to find sustenance that will fill their souls, but often in wrong places. I wonder how many of us are like this bird at times in our lives.

No matter what our needs or efforts, if they are expended in the wrong place or with the wrong focus, tree leaves cannot be turned into sustaining flowers, nor can the poisonous offerings of the world provide nutrition for the soul. Heavenly influence and blessing cannot be found in the adversary's design of imitations to fool our senses, providing not only empty calories for spiritual need, but also consumptions that are corruptive. Often, we are infected with poisons that drain health and life from our souls. Some experience the devastation of entrapment, without realizing what has occurred until and unless they look to the Savior, turning to Him, our source of spiritual nourishment and life.

Jesus Christ is the only source of truth, light, and love in our world. Coming to know Him and feel His love will fill our souls as we seek sustenance from the scriptures, writings of modern-day apostles and prophets, through prayer and the desire for heavenly gifts, even the Gift of the Holy Ghost.

Discipleship is a journey, one we take following Jesus Christ as our guide, example, and our Lord. In doing this we certainly meet the requirements of being a disciple, as we become converted followers of Christ. With the receipt of this blessing from Christ, perhaps our situation will be much like that of the sons of Mosiah, as recorded in the Book of Mormon, after they had been visited by an angel and embraced the truth.

> *Now these sons of Mosiah were with Alma at the time the angel first appeared unto him; therefore Alma did rejoice exceedingly to see his brethren, and what added more to his joy, they were still his brethren in the Lord; yea, and **they had waxed strong in the knowledge of the truth; for they were men of a sound understanding and they had searched the scriptures diligently, that they might know the word of God*** (Alma 17:2, emphasis added).

With the receipt of truth and a genuine desire to implement it in our lives, our discipleship will become evident in the decisions we make and how we live, desiring more truth, anxious to embrace all sacred sources and turning to the scriptures as Mosiah's sons did. Our steps will then be on the "covenant path," that path we entered through our baptism into the Church of Jesus Christ of Latter-Day Saints, taking Christ's name upon us. In this journey of discipleship we are being guided nearer to the Savior and inherit in that journey our souls will be filled with truth and light—divine nourishment for the soul, providing protection from the adversary's efforts at corruption.

Ponder on the Apostle Peter's relationship with the Savior and imagine yourself having his experiences in coming to know and love Jesus Christ, especially the experience that follows in the Introduction to this work, when Christ showed Himself once again to the apostles after the resurrection.

As you read, it will become apparent that I capitalize eternal life (Eternal Life), referencing this gift that Father gives the righteous in order to receive the sacred quality of life He has.

Atonement is an act of reconciliation between God and men which was performed by Jesus Christ, an act of sacrifice and blessing. It is essential to the purification and progression of Father's children. I capitalize it, having a special place in my heart and testimony.

Where Father and Christ dwell, I call "Home," because of the loving feelings it brings to my heart, the sanctity of its existence, and being so much more than a house or home in mortality. However, our homes should be consecrated for the receipt and embracing of the gospel and as a place of sacred preparation and protection that is ongoing to help make us ready for our return Home.

One other note. A prior book I have written, *Becometh As a Child,* supplied most of the information I have included that comes from King Benjamin's instruction to his people in the Book of Mormon, Mosiah chapters 2-4. I feel that this counsel, along with Peter's experience with Christ following His resurrection have great value when considered together.

INTRODUCTION

———⋘∘⟡∘⋙———

This is now the third time that Jesus shewed himself to his disciples, after that he was risen from the dead (John 21:14).

Simon Peter saith unto them, I go a fishing. They say unto him, We also go with thee.

But when the morning was now come, Jesus stood on the shore: but the disciples knew not that it was Jesus.

Then Jesus saith unto them, Children, have ye any meat: They answered him, No.

And he said unto them, Cast the net on the right side of the ship, and ye shall find. They cast therefore, and now they were not able to draw it for the multitude of fishes.

As soon then as they were come to land, they saw a fire of coals there, and fish laid thereon, and bread.

Jesus saith unto them, Bring of the fish which ye have now caught.

Simon Peter went up, and drew the net to land full of great fishes, an hundred and fifty and three: and for all there were so many, yet was not the net broken.

Jesus saith unto them, Come and dine. And none of the disciples durst ask him, Who art thou? knowing that it was the Lord.

So when they had dined, Jesus saith to Simon Peter, Simon, son of Jonas, Lovest thou me more than these (John 21: 3-6, 9-12, 15)?

CHAPTER 1

⊸∘℃⟋⟍⊃∘⊱

PETER'S AFFIRMATION

Peter answered the Lord's question, *Lovest thou me more than these* (the fish), in this way. *Yea, Lord; thou knowest that I love thee* (John 21:15). Jesus Christ did know that about Peter and responded with *Feed my lambs.* Do you wonder what was going through Peter's mind at this moment?

Peter likely had some background of instruction from the Old Testament regarding sheep or lambs that might have caused him to ponder; perhaps the story of Abraham and the instruction he received from God to offer Isaac as a sacrifice and then a ram as a substitute; the institution of the Passover; other sacrificial rites; Isaiah's prophecy of the Messiah feeding His flock like a shepherd, gathering, carrying, and leading His lambs. The context from these scriptural experiences must have provided some thoughtful connections as Peter attempted to understand what Jesus was asking and instructing. He may also have thought about the Savior's personal instruction to him as Christ and the apostles celebrated and observed the Passover before the crucifixion.

And the Lord said, Simon, Simon, behold, Satan hath desired to have you, that he may sift you as wheat:

1

But I have prayed for thee, that thy faith fail not: and when thou art converted, strengthen thy brethren (Luke 22:31-32).

Certainly, Christ had Peter's attention at that sacred gathering with a warning and instruction about going forward. All of this disciple's spiritual background may have played quickly within his mind, as he was asked a second time, *Simon, son of Jonas, lovest thou me?* Anxious to respond clearly, but with concerned surprise, Peter answered,

> *Thou knowest that I love thee. He saith unto him, Feed my sheep.*
>
> *He saith unto him the third time, Simon, son of Jonas, lovest thou me: Peter was grieved because he said unto him the third time, Lovest thou me: And he said unto him, Lord, thou knowest all things; thou knowest that I love thee. Jesus saith unto him, Feed my sheep* (John 21:16-17).

Peter was obviously troubled. Ponder. Put yourself in Peter's place. You have testified of your love for the Savior with His first question. How would you have felt with the second and the third? Would you feel that your love for Jesus was being called into question, that He was concerned that you really didn't answer truthfully or accurately?

Would you have understood what Christ taught following Peter's answers? After three successive questions with instruction, you likely would have understood as Peter must have, how important this work is that he was given and that his love for Christ must be preeminent over everything else. The path of discipleship was becoming clearer and undoubtedly concerns and confusion were transforming into truth and faith that would be needed for Peter to accomplish the great work that he was being given responsibility for.

Peter was impetuous, even daring, but certainly not yet the disciple and leader that Jesus knew he could be and must become. With a sword he attempted to protect Jesus when they were confronted in the Garden of Gethsemane. He followed Jesus to the castle of the high priest. These were acts of daring and love. But, when confronted at the high priest's residence about being a disciple of Jesus or knowing Him, he denied three times.

Jesus knew Peter through and through. He knew his weaknesses and strengths, Peter's fearlessness and its apparently negative companion of fearfulness. These three questions, though appearing to question Peter's loyalty and love, likely plumbed the reaches of Peter's soul and confirmed for Peter more about the priority and composition of his love, as well as the work to be done, all in that very short exchange.

He truly loved Jesus Christ. The calling of this question likely solidified for him the nature and importance of love, expressing it to his Lord who would know of its truthfulness. Peter began to realize with clarity what Jesus Christ was instructing him to do, to teach, preach, and testify of the Savior and gospel truths to all of God's children and lead them to the Son of God, now in the physical absence of the Savior. From that time forward, Peter progressed to become the man that the Lord wanted him to be.

What love filled questions have you fielded or decided upon in life? Often, we use "love" in place of "like" or "appreciate." Can you hear yourself saying, "I love that food," or "I love that whatever much more than the other one." Examining comparisons and responding using the term love is something that probably most of us do frequently in our lives. Answering using love likely establishes the intensity of our choice. However, these personal choices may carry little weight regarding the value we place on selections that define who we are, what we believe, and how we will live our lives.

In all likelihood, we all will be asked that same question in different ways, but in the nature of the inquiry that Jesus posed to Peter. With all the different times, stages, locations, and activities in our lives, we may be surprised at the asking of the question, or we may not recognize it at first, but the question will be asked. It might be as simple as, *Lovest thou me? Keep my commandments.* Our responses are as essential as Peter's. How would you honestly answer Christ's question right now? Do your thoughts and the decisions you make every day support you in saying,

Thou knowest I love thee. Do you feel there is a need in your life to make changes, so that your answer would be comparable to Peter's? You have been called to discipleship. Will you take the journey?

The enormity of the calling Peter had received, accepted, and the responsibility that was now his to take the gospel to all of Father's children, to feed Christ's sheep, must have weighed heavily upon his mind and heart in a way incomprehensible to most of us. Perhaps we have experienced in a small way what he felt as we have attempted to follow the Savior and bless the lives of our family members and others, a smaller world, but just as essential.

The test of love, loyalty, and obedience was a real one and required the exercise of faith, perhaps more completely than at any other time in Peter's relationship with the Savior; even from the time when Christ invited Andrew and him to *Follow me, and I will make you fishers of men* (Matthew 4:19). Jesus Christ had completed His mortal mission. He would not be in their physical presence as He had been, but all was prepared for the spiritual connection needed and the ability to go forward.

Peter would now be called upon to give leadership to those called to be apostles and others serving in the entire church, for all of the world. Fearfulness was purged from his being by the embracing of faith in Jesus Christ, recognizing Him as the Savior, and his love for Him. Did Peter love fishing, (even though it was central to his prior life and comfort zone), more than the Savior? The answer now was obviously "no!"

CHAPTER 2

⟡⟡⟡

THE INVITATION AND THE CALL

Again the next day after John (the Baptist) *stood, and two of his disciples;*

And looking upon Jesus as he walked, he saith, Behold the Lamb of God!

And the two disciples heard him speak, and they followed Jesus.

Then Jesus turned, and saw them following, and saith unto them, What seek ye? They said unto him, Rabbi, (which is to say, being interpreted, Master,) where dwellest thou?

He saith unto them, **Come and see.** *They came and saw where he dwelt, and abode with him that day: for it was about the tenth hour.*

One of the two which heard John speak, and followed him, was Andrew, Simon Peter's brother.

He first findeth his own brother Simon, and saith unto him, **We have found the Messias, which is, being interpreted, the Christ** (John 1:35-41, emphasis added).

And he brought him to Jesus. *And when Jesus beheld him, he said, Thou art Simon the son of Jona: thou shalt be called Cephas, which is, by interpretation, a seer, or a stone. And they* *were fishermen. **And they straightway left all, and followed Jesus** (JST John 1:42, Joseph Smith translation, emphasis added).*

Peter was introduced to Jesus Christ by an invitation that came from Andrew, his brother, and Andrew was invited to "come and see" by Christ.

Responding to the invitation by Jesus Christ, Peter, Andrew and the other 10 disciples followed their curiosity and a spirit of wonder to come and personally meet the Savior. Biddings to come meet Him, to know Him, follow Him, and receive all the blessings Father has for His children have been made from Adam's day until now. Christ personally made these invitations and continues to make invitations to "come and see" through the Spirit and those who have aligned their lives with Him as disciples. Consider these expressions from the scriptures.

*Ho, every one that thirsteth, **come ye** to the waters* . . . (living waters or Christ, Isaiah 55:1, emphasis added).

***Come unto me,** all ye that labour and are heavy laden, and I will give you rest.*

Take my yoke upon you, and learn of me; for I am meek and lowly in heart: and ye shall find rest unto your souls. (Matthew 11:28-29, emphasis added).

*But Jesus said, Suffer little children, and **forbid them not, to come unto me:** for of such is the kingdom of heaven* (Matthew 19:14, emphasis added).

*And Jesus said unto them, I am the bread of life: **he that cometh to me** shall never hunger; and **he that believeth on me** shall never thirst* (John 6:35, emphasis added).

*. . . for he (the Lord) doeth that which is good among the children of men; and he doeth nothing save it be plain unto the children of men; and he **inviteth them all** to come unto him and partake of his goodness; and he denieth none that come unto him, black and white, bond and free, male and female; and he*

remembereth the heathen; and all are alike unto God, both Jew and Gentile (2 Nephi 26:33, emphasis added).

Therefore **come unto me** *and be ye saved; for verily I say unto you, that except ye shall keep my commandments, which I have commanded you at this time, ye shall in no case enter into the kingdom of heaven* (3 Nephi 12:20, emphasis added).

While Lehi and his family were traveling through the wilderness, as guided by the Lord and recorded in the Book of Mormon, he received a vision of the Tree of Life which he related to his family. Nephi, at a later time, was also permitted to see what his father saw (1 Nephi 8, 11, 12:16-18, 15:22-29).

The vision expressed the invitation that comes to all of God's children to come to Jesus Christ by making the decisions that put the person on the sacred path that will guide her or him to the Tree of Life, which is a representation of the love of God. Its fruit is Eternal Life. Keeping the commandments and bringing forth works of righteousness are our responsibility all along the path. We are free to decide, but if we choose not to make our way, justice will prevail and Father's gifts will be withheld.

Wherefore, the wicked are rejected from the righteous, and also from that tree of life, whose fruit is most precious and most desirable above all other fruits; yea, and it is the greatest of all the gifts of God (1 Nephi 15:36).

And, if you, keep my commandments and endure to the end you shall have eternal life, which gift is the greatest of all the gifts of God (D&C 14:7).

The following instruction from the prophet Moroni details in glorious language the outcome that each one of us can receive, if we accept the invitation to come to Jesus Christ. We must follow the counsel we are given, even as Peter, turning to the Savior with all of our minds and hearts.

Yea, **come unto Christ, and be perfected in him,** *and deny yourselves of all ungodliness; and if ye shall deny yourselves of all ungodliness, and love God with all your might, mind and strength, then is his grace sufficient for you, that by his grace ye may be perfect in Christ; and if by the grace of God ye are perfect in Christ, ye can in nowise deny the power of God.*

And again, if ye by the grace of God are perfect in Christ, and deny not his power, **then are ye sanctified in Christ by the grace of God,** *through the shedding of the blood of Christ, which is in the covenant of the Father unto the remission of your sins, that ye become holy, without spot* (Moroni 10:32-33, emphasis added).

The disciples accepted the invitation made by Jesus Christ without all of the scriptural evidence that we have in front of us. They likely did not know where accepting the invitation would take them, even as we do not know when we accept. Receiving and acting on the invitation led them through a sense of awakening, coming to know who Christ is and who they are, followed by the miracle of conversion, and they became witnesses of the fulfilment of prophecy regarding the coming of the Messiah.

Eleven of the original twelve accepted calls of service and thus began the ongoing mission throughout the world, until the end of time to gather those of Father's children who desire to return to Him. They received priesthood callings as apostles, having the responsibility to bear witness of the Savior and to lead and direct the affairs of the Savior's church following His return to heaven.

John describes the evidence of the invitation and call by saying *they straightway left all, and followed Jesus.* Matthew depicts what took place in this way.

And he saith unto them, Follow me, and I will make you fishers of men. And they straightway left their nets, and followed him (Matthew 4:19-20).

Such is the Savior's power with those willing to "come and see." The honest in heart will make changes in their lives, often immediately filled with a desire to follow Him. That power was evidenced in the meridian of time with these and other disciples and is evidenced today as the Spirit invites the honest in heart to become true disciples of Jesus Christ. That is the invitation given to you.

This pattern of invitation, following, and then receiving a call to service is the process by which all of Father's children are introduced to Jesus Christ and the gospel. The prophet Alma in the New World explained traveling the path in this way.

Behold, he sendeth an invitation unto all men, for the arms of mercy are extended towards them and He saith: Repent, and I will receive you.

Yea, he saith: Come unto me and ye shall partake of the fruit of the tree of life; yea, ye shall eat and drink of the bread and the waters of life freely;

Yea, come unto me and bring forth works of righteousness, and ye shall not be hewn down and cast into the fire— (Alma 5:33-35).

Alma was high priest over the Church and also served as the chief judge in the land. He gave up the judgeship to spend all of his time among the people, bearing witness of the word of God. He began first on this quest in the land of Zarahemla. In the midst of revealing to the people their sins, he made this invitation as recorded above, explaining the blessings that come following repentance and continuous striving for righteousness.

To *eat and drink of the bread and the waters of life freely* is to receive Jesus Christ as our Lord and Savior and to love Him more than the temporary gifts and pleasures of mortal life. If we come and turn to Him, making Christ the foundation of our lives, the focus then of our daily righteous efforts are as important as eating and drinking for the physical body. We will have all that is needful for us to receive all the blessings Father has for His children.

If we accept this invitation and come unto Christ and endure to the end, the role, the reason for mortality will have been fulfilled for us as we give Him our loyalty and our lives for the blessing of our families and others, holding sacred in our hearts that He is the bread of life.

Commensurate with this invitation, if we are willing to receive it, the Spirit will witness to us of truth and seek and encourage our attention to be focused continually toward the Source of Truth and Light. The invitation may come seemingly in many different ways, but it will come even in these last chaotic days.

What experiences, impressions or thoughts have occurred in your life that have invited and encouraged you to turn to the Savior? How did you respond to them? Did you believe and embrace them or casually turn from them to other worldly invitations? If you turned away, what experience provided a strong enough invitation to turn back and seek the Light? How has your life changed by turning back and striving to become a disciple? Are you where you want to be on the covenant path. Are invitations to progress continuing to come to you frequently? If Peter was having similar experiences to the ones you are having, how do you think he would respond to them?

Paul, an apostle of the Lord Jesus Christ in the meridian of time, prophesied regarding the last days, certainly the time we are now in. Consider his words to see if they correspond with what you know of the attitudes and works, unfortunately, of many of God's children in our day.

This know also, that in the last days perilous times shall come.
For men shall be lovers of their own selves, covetous, boasters,
proud, blasphemers, disobedient to parents, unthankful, unholy,

Without natural affection, trucebreakers, false accusers, incontinent, fierce, despisers of those that are good,

Traitors, heady, highminded, lovers of pleasures more than lovers of God;

Having a form of godliness, but denying the power thereof; from such turn away (2 Timothy 3:1- 5).

The sins of this generation are not new and are found throughout time and around the world. At the time of Noah, as we know from the scriptures, the world was terribly evil. Here is how Moses described the wickedness in Genesis 6:5.

And God saw that the wickedness of man was great in the earth, and that every imagination of the thoughts of his heart was only evil continually.

In response, God covered the earth with water and only eight people were saved, all were Noah's family.

Paul's description in 2 Timothy is sobering. The prophesies concerning this time in history are vital to us, because this is our day. Sins will not be excused just because they are so prevalent around us. Committing sin continues to be a very personal choice, especially since each child was given the Light of Christ (conscience) at birth to provide spiritual balance, preparing us to receive the gospel from Jesus Christ. If we have received the gospel, arrived at the age of accountability, and desire to be faithful, the blessing of the Gift of the Holy Ghost will be ours by receiving that gift following baptism.

If we do not align our lives with truth, repenting of our sins, our relationship with Father and the Savior and our worthiness to return Home and be in Their presence will be negatively and painfully impacted. The Gift of the Holy Ghost will not be given or his companionship will be withdrawn if we are not repentant. Being left alone, without the Spirit, is an outcome that the adversary puts significant effort to. We need that protection.

11

In Noah's time God cleansed the earth with water. At the end, Malachi's prophesy explains that the world will be cleansed by fire.

> *For, behold, the day cometh, that shall burn as an oven; and all the proud, yea, and all that do wickedly, shall be stubble; and the day that cometh shall burn them up, saith the Lord of hosts, that it shall leave them neither root nor branch* (Malachi 4:1).

To be burned as stubble leaves a very clear picture of having no value, no future, and being bereft of all the blessings this world was designed to give.

From the Lord's instruction to Adam and Eve and others by His own voice, by the visitation of angels, and the whispering of the Spirit throughout time, the "invitation" has gone out and will continue to impress on individual souls the necessity to turn to the Savior until all of God's children have had the opportunity to turn to Christ. To not do so is terrible to comprehend.

How is it that all of Father's children are or will be capable of knowing the truth of His and Jesus Christ's word? Christ was chosen before the world was to be the Savior and the only One who can save us.

> *Know ye not that ye are the temple of God, and that the Spirit of God dwelleth in you* (1 Corinthians 3:16)?
>
> *For the word of the Lord is truth, and whatsoever is truth is light, and whatsoever is light is Spirit, even the Spirit of Jesus Christ.*
>
> *And the Spirit giveth light to every man that cometh into the world* (D&C 84:45-46, emphasis added).

These scriptures make it perfectly clear that each of Father's children has been given the inborn tools to recognize truth when it is presented, in every age, whether on this side of the veil or on the spirit side, no matter what their culture, religion, language, or family relationship is.

The Spirit will enlighten or guide each of God's children **if the person will listen to the invitation and give heed to the Spirit.**

Knowing that we have the capacity to recognize truth, what can we do to be proactive, rather than passive in the mortal experience that is supposed to prepare us to return Home? How can we receive truth despite the worldly influences that are not supportive in its receipt, but often are adversarial?

> *Draw near unto me and I will draw near unto; seek me diligently and ye shall find me; ask, and ye shall receive; knock, and it shall be opened unto you* (D&C 88:63).

The Lord has clearly prepared the way and commanded that we need to reach out to Him and be diligent in doing so. If we do, He will reach out to us. Is that it? Is that all that is required, just to ask? At least that is the beginning. The prophet Nephi in the Book of Mormon has written prophetic counsel that will help in answering this question.

> *And he cometh into the world that he may save all men if they will **hearken** unto his voice* (2 Nephi 9:21, emphasis added).

There is that similar language that instructs us to hearken or to listen and give heed to what is said. We should not be surprised that in order to receive what the Lord has to offer, we must listen and be obedient to His instruction. Nephi, later in his writings, gives more definition of what our asking of the Lord must or not include.

> *Wherefore, my beloved brethren, I know that if ye shall follow the Son, with **full purpose of heart,** acting no hypocrisy and no deception before God, but with real intent, repenting of your sins, witnessing unto the Father that ye are willing to take upon you the name of Christ, by baptism—yea, by following your Lord and your Savior down into the water, according to his word, behold, then shall ye receive the Holy Ghost; yea, then cometh the baptism*

of fire and of the Holy Ghost; and then can ye speak with the tongue of angels, and shout praises unto the Holy One of Israel (2 Nephi 31:13, emphasis added).

Repentance, baptism, receiving the Gift of the Holy Ghost, open up the doors to truth and light, and a relationship with the Savior that will be close and transforming in its nature. This instruction was given to Nephi by Jesus Christ. Nephi also heard a voice from the Father, saying: *Yea, the words of my Beloved are true and faithful. He that endureth to the end, the same shall be saved* (2 Nephi 31:15).

The meaning is very clear regarding what "asking and hearkening" requires of us. "Full purpose of heart" defines that we are genuine or honest in our request, anxious to know and understand and being willing to expend the energy and effort to do so. It means we are willing to hear and accept whatever is revealed to us, even if it is not what we thought we wanted. We commit or covenant to embrace all that we are instructed in and make it part of who we are, because we are asking without hypocrisy or deception.

Since a covenant is an agreement between two parties, we are agreeing to follow the Savior, to be baptized in His name and if we do so the Lord agrees or promises to give us the Holy Ghost and a baptism of "fire and of the Holy Ghost" will follow. That baptism of fire signifies a cleansing, being purified and prepared to become and do all that the Lord desires of us, even as we use fire in a similar way with earthly elements.

We are promised that we will be able to speak with the "tongue of angels" or in the language angels speak and be in a position to "shout praises unto the Holy One of Israel," the Savior, Jesus Christ. Perhaps you have felt the fulfillment of these in your life, feeling the desire to witness to others the truths of this instruction. The desire to shout praises of thanksgiving is a natural response to the outcomes of these gifts and may prompt us to witness to others these truths in different ways. Certainly, with this understanding, we will accept and fulfill any call we are given.

How are we to receive the Savior's instruction? the scriptures, Church attendance, the voices of prophets and apostles. Prayer is an obvious choice and the Holy Ghost will confirm the truths which are revealed. That is one of the missions or responsibilities of the Holy Ghost.

A caution was given to the prophet Moroni as recorded in the Book of Mormon by Jesus Christ regarding truth.

> *And whatsoever thing persuadeth men to do good is of me; for good cometh of none save it be of me. I am the same that leadeth men to all good; he that will not believe my words will not believe me—that I am; and he that will not believe me will not believe the Father who sent me. For behold . . ., I am the light, and the life, and the truth of the world* (Ether 4:12).

We must first believe the words of the Savior; for the Holy Ghost will confirm them if we are genuine in our desire to know the truth, to know that Jesus Christ is the Savior. If we do not, then we will not trust who Jesus Christ is. We will have effectively refused to receive instruction of what is required to be worthy to return Home. Having done this, we have refused to receive the greatest gift Father can bestow upon us, Eternal Life, the kind of life God, our Father in Heaven, has.

Becoming as a child is a foundational requirement of receiving the truth of our existence and potential, including the plan of salvation from the source of all truth and light, Jesus Christ.

> *Therefore, whoso repenteth and **cometh unto me as a little child,** him will I receive, for of such is the kingdom of God* (3 Nephi 9:22, emphasis added).

On this life pathway, which has become known in our day as the "covenant pathway," we are required to make promises and keep them as we never will graduate from being a child on this return Home. It is foundational in becoming a disciple of Jesus Christ and throughout our discipleship. We must always be in the position and attitude of anxiously receiving more truth and light, having committed to receive, embrace, and make it a part of our lives. This is what receiving and acting upon the "invitation" is and requires.

When we genuinely accept and follow through with the invitation, a call will follow, even as it did for Peter and other disciples. This "call" will embrace all that is part of living righteously and loving Christ with all our beings. Our lives must and will manifest our conversion and relationship with Jesus Christ, desiring to bless others. We will likely be given additional responsibilities as guided by the Spirit within the call to give service that is a genuine part of God's work.

CHAPTER 3

—⊸oᏟᔒᎲᎧo⊷—

GOD'S WORK IS OUR WORK

Knowing that we are Father's children, does it surprise you that the Savior has invited us to join Him in His work? Think about this. If Christ's work is to provide the opportunity, instruction, tutoring, example, leadership, sacred environment, saving ordinances, forgiveness, and clearly defined pathway for Home, would these be sign posts all along the journey? Doesn't it make sense that He would invite us to join in the effort with Him, so that we can become like Him, exercising our love for Him and all of Father's children? Certainly, that was what Jesus Christ was helping Peter to understand when He posed the same question to Peter three times, *lovest thou me?*

If we are to return Home and enjoy the quality life He has with responsibilities that mirror His in any way, when should we start the education we need now to be worthy and able? "Yesterday" doesn't sound soon enough. Let's take a small liberty and restate Moses 1:39 making it personal to us. *For behold, this is our work and blessing to assist in bringing to pass the eternal life of man and the glory of God.*

How do we begin? The scriptural record from Adam to our present day makes it very clear that we begin by being obedient and understanding all the whys is not prerequisite to doing it. To obey requires a sense of trust that our Savior knows what is best for us, even if we don't know

17

why. Isn't that a natural part of parent and child relationships in our temporal world? Oh, the value of childhood and the lessons available, lessons hopefully we are learning.

Is there a heavenly family corollary to our earthly family? Earthly parents strive to have us learn from them and put our lives in order to prepare for the future. Father requires the same. The Savior instructed the people in the new world to *come unto me with full purpose of heart* (3 Nephi 18:32). He promised spiritual healing for those who do. The prophet Mormon outlined this same instruction.

> *Nevertheless they did fast and pray oft, and did wax stronger and stronger in their humility, and firmer and firmer in the faith of Christ, unto the filling their souls with joy and consolation, yea, even to the purifying and the sanctification of their hearts, which sanctification cometh because of their yielding their hearts unto God* (Helaman 3:35).

The parallels between earthly and heavenly parentage do exist. Earthly parent responsibilities have been designed to follow the pattern set by our Father in His home and for us here on earth with love being a key component and ever-attending power.

"Full purpose of heart" is a necessary element of true obedience. When we are obedient, we open the door and windows to our soul so that God can share through invitation, inspiration, instruction, and experience the qualities and components that are integral to being a faithful child, prepared to progress on the covenant path leading to Eternal Life. We lift our desires and efforts higher to be more in tune with Christ.

The blessing of associating with Father, the Savior, and those who have given Them their loyalty began in our Heavenly Home and continues here with instruction and requirements within our temporal and spiritual capabilities. The anticipation is that these are growing to become progressive capabilities, gaining strength and understanding beyond where we began in our premortal Home.

Obedience has the power to influence growth into Godly attitudes and aptitudes, if we turn to God with full purpose, yielding our hearts unto Him. If we don't, we won't fully flower with necessary attributes and desires, therefore hindering us in maturation and drawing nearer unto Christ. Drawing near is necessary to be worthy of returning Home and being in His presence. Spiritual maturation will be evidenced by our strivings to follow this instruction from Jesus Christ given in the Sermon on the Mount.

> *Ye have heard that it hath been said, Thou shalt love thy neighbour, and hate thine enemy.*
> *But I say unto you, Love your enemies, bless them that curse you, do good to them that hate you and pray for them which despitefully use you, and persecute you;*
> *That ye may be the children of your Father which is in heaven: for he maketh his sun to rise on the evil and on the good, and sendeth rain on the just and on the unjust* (Matthew 5:43-45).

As is evidenced by obedience and turning our hearts to the Savior, we will be endowed with the desire and ability to make His work our work. How far can our abilities progress? Consider this scripture given to Joseph Smith regarding members of the Church of Jesus Christ of Latter-Day Saints in Missouri.

> *For they were set to be a light unto the world, and to be the saviors of men* (D&C 103:9).

By implication, all of God's children, through obedience, are to be "saviors of men." We are to follow in the footsteps of Jesus Christ and bless the lives of others as He would bless them, striving within our abilities, following His commandments, and using the gifts we have been given to do so.

These two sources of power are essential for God's work to be our work, **love** and **faith**.

... Thou shalt love the Lord thy God with all thy heart, and with all thy soul, and with all thy mind.

This is the first and great commandment.

And the second is like unto it, Thou shalt love thy neighbour as thy self (Matthew 22:37-39).

Remember that without faith you can do nothing ... (D&C 8:10).

And if you have not faith, hope, and charity, you can do nothing (D&C 18:19).

Charity is love, the pure love of Christ (Moroni 7:47).

Simply, this is our work. The instruction, tools, and power are all available to us. We have been called to discipleship and will be authorized to do it and fulfill the "call" as we follow the Savior.

CHAPTER 4

⇌∘⟡∘⇌

PETER'S EDUCATION

At the "personal interview" which appears to have been not very private, when Christ asked Peter about his love for Him, His questions and instruction brought to a focus the understanding of the leadership that would be required of Peter and the example that others would need to see from him with the end of Christ's mortal ministry. This earlier sacred instruction from the Savior, which occurred at the Last Supper, may have been on Peter's mind at that time.

And the Lord said, Simon, Simon, behold Satan hath desired to have you, that he may sift you as wheat (Luke 22:31).

Likely, Peter gained greater understanding that Satan's desire is not passive but is an active opposition with actions and varied efforts designed to sew corruption in Peter's soul, using many imaginative ways to access Peter's weaknesses as needed. Later, before the awakening of a new day and before the Savior's crucifixion, Peter denied knowing or being a follower of Christ three times (Matthew 14:66-72).

Perhaps, we can appreciate the sorrow and shame he may have felt after responding to fear and realizing with clarity the reality and importance of Christ's warning only hours earlier. The call to service he received following the Lord's resurrection, with the responsibilities and sacrifices that would be required were undoubtably coming into focus. He had been watching and learning directly from the Savior's service and quiet moments of instruction and reflection that undoubtedly occurred throughout Christ's ministry and Peter's companionship.

Certainly, Peter sought repentance and learned that through the Savior's forgiveness and his own desires he could continue seeking to be faithful, trustworthy, and complete the call he was given. Following the warning, Christ revealed His effort to provide protection, support, and instruction. What a blessing it is for us to recognize the importance of prayer by having witnesses of Christ offering prayer to our Father in Peter's behalf and for others.

> *But I have prayed for thee, that thy faith fail not: and when thou art converted, strengthen thy brethren* (Luke 22:32).

On the cross, Christ prayed for those who were responsible for His crucifixion. A love for them despite what they were doing is so evident. What does that reveal to you about Christ?

> *Then said Jesus, Father, forgive them; for they know not what they do* (Luke 23:34).

Following His resurrection, Christ appeared to the people in the New World and offered this prayer on behalf of the twelve disciples He had chosen and those who would believe in their testimonies.

> *Father, I thank thee that thou hast given the Holy Ghost unto these whom I have chosen; and it is because of their belief in me that I have chosen them out of the world.,*
> *Father, I pray thee that thou wilt give the Holy Ghost unto all them that shall believe in their words* (3 Nephi 19:20-21).

If prayer was important to the Savior, to the Son of God, then there is no question about how important and valuable prayer is in our relationship with Father. We must do as Christ did, calling upon Father in humility, faith, and trust. We offer prayer in the name of Christ, which aligns us with all three of the Godhead, Father, Son, and Holy Ghost, as inspiration comes from the Holy Ghost or Spirit regarding what we should pray for and the answers we receive, if we humbly and meekly seek it.

Peter was the Savior's chief apostle and blessings were given according to his needs and call to service. However, Jesus Christ will do no less for us, forgiving our sins as we repent and strive to be faithful, being given blessings to fulfill the stewardships we are given. The instruction in this specific record from Luke was said for Peter's benefit to provide him an important warning, but also knowledge of Christ's assistance, and what was expected of him. Ponder on what was said and you will likely realize that the instruction and warning seem to aptly apply to our lives as well.

Satan's Desire to Control Us

Satan has been the opposition to Father's plan for His children from the beginning. His opposition is of serious concern as righteousness, progression, and eternal reward unto Eternal Life are all at risk for those who do not align their lives with Father's will. Satan exerts all his power to deceive, confuse, corrupt, and destroy. The Plan of Salvation is in place and the individual lives of Father's children are at risk, depending on the decisions they make.

Satan is skilled at his chosen craft of deception, deceit and inspiring sin. The Savior's portrayal of Satan's desire to "sift Peter as wheat," was a descriptive analogy that likely struck Peter with clarity and concern as he would likely know what was required in the threshing and sifting of grain. This comparison must have made a powerful impression upon him, as he continued in the process of conversion that was not yet fully flowered. Being sifted sounds terrible, even in our culture.

Christ's Prayer

The Savior's very act of praying for Peter bears a witness that should awaken us to the power that is intrinsic to it and the essential communication that prayer is. When in the New World, Christ taught the multitude that gathered at His arrival and commanded that their little children be brought and seated around Him.

> *And it came to pass that when they had all been brought, and Jesus stood in the midst, he commanded the multitude that they should kneel down upon the ground.*
>
> *And it came to pass that when they had knelt upon the ground, Jesus groaned within himself, and said: Father, I am troubled because of the wickedness of the people of the house of Israel.*
>
> *And when he had said these words, he himself also knelt upon the earth; and behold he prayed unto the Father, and the things which he prayed cannot be written, and the multitude did bear record who heard him.*
>
> *And after this manner do they bear record: The eye hath never seen, neither hath the ear heard, before, so great and marvelous things as we saw and heard Jesus speak unto the Father;*
>
> *And no tongue can speak, neither can there be written by any man, neither can the hearts of men conceive so great and marvelous things as we both saw and heard Jesus speak; and no one can conceive of the joy which filled our souls at the time we heard him pray for us unto the Father* (3 Nephi 17:13-17).

With this tender example of The Only Begotten of the Father, praying for the children and their parents who surrounded Him, can we even be tempted to discount the influence and necessity of prayer in our lives and the need to pray for others?

What a tragedy it is for anyone to discount the power and need of prayer by saying that "this is the Son of God who prayed and not one of us. We will never have a powerful experience like that."

It would be glorious to have a similar experience with Christ in our lives. Actually, we can have prayer experiences that have a deep and powerful impact upon us through the Holy Ghost, if we turn to the Savior with full purpose of heart. Full purpose of heart, you will read it many times in reference to our relationship with Father and Christ, for it is a requirement in order to receive all the gifts that Father has for us. It means we are not acting in hypocrisy or deception, that we are genuine in our desires and efforts, expending our energy and abilities, while striving to love and obey.

It is vital that we pray with faith, trusting our prayers will be heard. Blessings will be given according to our needs and Father's will, even instruction with a similar power to awaken, confirm, and empower our faithful efforts.

> *Yea, and cry unto God for all thy support; yea, let all thy doings be unto the Lord, and whithersoever thou goes let it be in the Lord; yea, let all they thoughts be directed unto the Lord; yea, let the affections of thy heart be placed upon the Lord forever.*
>
> *Counsel with the Lord in all thy doings, and he will direct thee for good; yea, when thou liest down at night lie down unto the Lord, that he may watch over you in your sleep; and when thou risest in the morning let thy heart be full of thanks unto God; and if ye do these things, ye shall be lifted up at the last day* (Alma 37:36-37).

There can be no question about the necessity of prayer in our lives, including when and how often genuine prayer should be offered.

This instruction given by Alma to his son, Helaman, is as valid and needed today as it was then. Consider this profound instruction and promise given by the Savior as he taught in the New World.

Behold, verily, verily, I say unto you, ye must watch and pray always lest ye enter into temptation; for Satan desireth to have you, that he may sift you as wheat.

Therefore ye must always pray unto the Father in my name;

And whatsoever ye shall ask the Father in my name, which is right, believing that ye shall receive, behold it shall be given unto you.

Pray in your families unto the Father, always in my name, that your wives and your children may be blessed (3 Nephi 18:18-21).

Christ's instructions to this multitude contain the same warning as given to Peter with directives on the application of prayer in their lives; the same application we have in our day. Herein is direction for personal and family prayer, a testimony to the converting and efficacious power of prayer.

Unfailing Faith

Christ prayed that Peter's faith would not fail. Unfailing faith is considered certain or dependable. The affairs of Christ's kingdom on the earth could not be left with leadership that did not have the faith to weather all the storms of life and withstand the efforts of the adversary to destroy it. The Lord's guidance was and is essential.

Faith must be taught to all those desiring to know if Jesus Christ is the Savior of the world. The Apostle Paul said:

Now faith is the substance of things hoped for, the evidence of things not seen (Hebrews 11:1).

So then faith cometh by hearing, and hearing by the word of God (Romans 10:17).

Hope doesn't have a physical presence. It can't be seen, touched by a hand, or given as a gift from one person to another. However, hope has place in the heart, in the soul, and in these locations gifts can be given and received that are beyond the understanding of men, because they are gifts of the Spirit from God.

> *But the natural man receiveth not the things of the Spirit of God: for they are foolishness unto him: neither can he know them, because they are spiritually discerned* (1 Corinthians 2:14).

To desire sacred gifts, receive them, and recognize them, requires turning from the influence of the world (natural man) to that of the Spirit, exercising belief, which over time, plus experience and exercise, deepens and purifies into faith.

> *And now as I said concerning faith—faith is not to have a perfect knowledge of things; therefore if ye have faith ye hope for things which are not seen, which are true* (Alma 32:21).

Truth is revealed and confirmed by the Holy Ghost.

> *And now, I, Moroni, would speak somewhat concerning these things; I would show unto the world that faith is things which are hoped for and not seen; wherefore dispute not because ye see not, for ye receive no witness until after the trial of your faith* (Ether 12:6).

The investment in exercising belief and hope, leading unto faith, is far more than a casual approach or singular event in order to receive truth and have it confirmed by the Spirit. We must prove our sincerity, responsibility, and our willingness to put forth the effort with determination to receive that which is sacred.

The exercise of hope, obedience to commandments and instruction, and the willingness to do so, until we receive an answer (all of which evidences belief) is required for faith to grow. This is how it gains strength and becomes dependable for us in assisting the Lord in His work and for the salvation of our own souls. Faith begins and ends in

Jesus Christ. He is the source of all truth and light. It is this pathway that develops faith that will not fail.

It is impossible to successfully complete a trial of our faith and align ourselves with Father's will and not be filled with a love for Christ that transforms us. This love is transcendent to any mortal emotion.

Conversion

The process of being converted is to accept one belief in the place of another, even in place of "no belief." In Peter's situation, he must accept that Jesus Christ is the Son of God, the promised Redeemer, and that everything He did and taught was for the blessing of Father's children. Peter had been called and ordained with the other apostles to continue the work and organization of the Savior's church after His ascension. That conversion solidified him in becoming trustworthy with the power and responsibility to fulfill Jesus Christ's desires, even to the sacrifice of his own life. What may not be recognized is that conversion requires us to be as children, with faith and hope leading us to trust in the love and saving grace of the Lord.

> *And Jesus called a little child unto him, and set him in the midst of them,*
>
> *And said, Verily I say unto you, Except ye be converted, and become as little children, ye shall not enter into the kingdom of heaven.*
>
> *Whosoever therefore shall humble himself as this little child, the same is greatest in the kingdom of heaven.*
>
> *And whoso shall receive one such little child in my name receiveth me* (Matthew 18:2-5).

Strengthening Others

> *. . . I have prayed for thee, that thy faith fail not:* **and when thou art converted, strengthen thy brethren** (Luke 22:32, emphasis added).

Strengthen thy brethren. Feed my lambs. Feed my sheep. The call to sanctifying service is clear. We have examined these two verses of instruction from the Savior, Luke 22:31-32, in separate parts to attempt to understand all of the meaning that it may have had for Peter and certainly for us in our current station in life.

However, regarding the command to strengthen his brethren, perhaps the Savior's instruction should now be examined in entirety with the other prominent parts of the instruction.

> *And the Lord said, Simon, Simon, behold, Satan hath desired to have you, that he may sift you as wheat:*
> *But I have prayed for thee, that thy faith fail not: and when thou art converted, strengthen thy brethren* (Luke 22:31-32).

Christ illuminated Satan's efforts to control and corrupt Peter. Following the crucifixion, Peter knew his fear had overcome faith when he denied being a disciple of Christ three times as the Lord was being interrogated in that illegal high priest court. Peter hadn't stood with courage as a friend, a disciple, or as one who loved Him. It is likely that this personal "failure" was eventually known by all the apostles. Shame may have been a cloud he struggled to come out from under. As difficult as it is to comprehend the weight of that failure, the pain that filled his soul must have been a burden Peter didn't know how he would resolve. Sorrow. Shame. Pain. Love.

To hear from the Savior at that last supper together with the other apostles that Christ had prayed for Peter must have filled his soul immediately with love and thanksgiving. He may have, at that time, recognized the healing gift of mercy, that he would surely experience later as he struggled and repented of his fear. A prayer for unfailing faith would give pause and reflection regarding all that had happened, filling a soul hungry for forgiveness, peace, faith, and hope, with the understanding that all will be well.

When thou art converted—those were words of instruction, intended to be received with loyalty, determination, and recommitted faith to become who the Lord wanted him to be. The standard of righteous living must be met in order to *strengthen thy brethren*. That burden would begin to fill his mind and heart. The Only Begotten of The Father wanted him to continue and by example, effort, and sacrificing all he had to give to strengthen his brethren in their quorum and all those who would come into the Church, even all the children of God.

He would go on to teach, encourage, mentor, bear witness, and love all of Father's children. Peter's lessons are fully applicable to each of us as we all deal with the challenges of mortality, which Peter was not excused from, and the efforts of the adversary to disrupt our walk on the covenant path. We are certainly not alone. We should be praying for each other, exercising love that is without boundaries that includes all of Father's children. This is beginning to love as Christ loves.

CHAPTER 5

—◦◦◦◦—

THE PRINCIPLE OF ONENESS

One of my family's favorite places to visit when our children were young was Mission Bay in Southern California. We had a favorite RV park that was near the beach. In every camp spot, we always needed some place to hang our towels and swimming suits to dry, so I would tie a rope to a neighboring tree and the other end to our trailer.

One day, we returned "home" and as we approached our laundry line, we could see a nearly continuous line of small black dots or objects on the rope that stretched from the tree to the trailer. After a few steps we discovered they were ants. We watched as they made their way inside the trailer to the various items of food in the cupboards and back out again. We didn't mind sharing, but that was a little much. I cut off their freeway to the food and then the challenge of cleanup began.

This illustration of the ants being one in purpose and effort, or oneness is not unusual or an isolated experience in our world. Can this simple example in nature also be symbolic of God's desire for His relationship with His children and for the way they live their lives?

We see this organization frequently in nature and examples of it in humanity. Group harmony developed from aligning individual efforts is impressive whether in ants or people. Somehow ants communicate

31

and align for the same purpose. Consider sports teams, work teams, organization goals and efforts, and family labor that unifies members at many levels of living, while preserving individual identities and characteristics.

Becoming one in righteous purpose and effort is a Godly principle and heavenly communication is given in several ways. Consider the Light of Christ, scriptures and personal instruction of the Spirit. However, as you read and ponder the following scriptures, it will become apparent that "oneness" has a depth beyond being only one in purpose and effort as understood by much of the world. The following principle is an essential part of becoming one as illustrated by these scriptures.

> ***I and my Father are one*** (John 10:30, emphasis added).
> *I say unto you, that this is my doctrine, and I bear record of it from the Father; and whoso believeth in me believeth in the Father also; and unto him will the Father bear record of me, for he will visit him with fire and with the Holy Ghost*
> *. . . and the Holy Ghost will bear record unto him of the Father and me;* ***for the Father, and I, and the Holy Ghost are one*** (3 Nephi 11:35-36, emphasis added).

Undoubtedly, the members of the Godhead being identified as "one" may be challenging to some as viewed in this temporal world, but never-the-less they are three independent Gods and the scriptures here teach the truth. As hard as that concept may be to understand for some, what about Father's children becoming one with Him and the Savior?

> *Whosoever shall confess that Jesus is the Son of God, God* ***dwelleth in him, and he in God*** (1 John 4:15, emphasis added).
> *And the Lord called his people Zion, because they were of* ***one heart and one mind***, *and dwelt in righteousness; and there was no poor among them* (Moses 7:18, emphasis added).

*And now Father, I pray unto thee for them, and also for all those who shall believe on their words, that they may believe in me, **that I may be in them as thou, Father, art in me, that we may be one** (3 Nephi 19:23, emphasis added).*

. . . Have ye not read, that he which made them at the beginning made them male and female,

*And said, for this cause shall a man leave father and mother, and shall cleave to his wife: and **they twain shall be one flesh?***

Wherefore they are no more twain, but one flesh (Matthew 19:4-6, emphasis added).

*That in the dispensation of the fulness of times he might **gather together in one** all things in Christ, both which are in heaven, and which are on earth; even in him (Ephesians 1:10).*

It should become apparent to our understanding of earth life, God's work, and our work that oneness is a godly principle. What a transcendent concept and how vital it is for us to get our "spiritual arms" around it with clarity and embrace it with all our being! The Apostle John, recording the Savior's Intercessory Prayer, which provides a distinct and profound understanding of the nature of oneness and potential application in our lives, documented this.

Neither pray I for these alone, but for them also which shall believe on me through their word;

That they all may be one; as thou, Father, art in me, and I in thee, that they also may be one in us: that the world may believe that thou hast sent me.

*And the glory which thou gavest me I have given them; **that they may be one, even as we are one:***

I in them, and thou in me, that they may be made perfect in one; and that the world may know that thou hast sent me, and hast loved them, as thou hast loved me (John 17:20-23, emphasis added).

Becoming one with the Savior suggests a depth that is beyond our current understanding. However, the Sacramental Prayers contain a promise within the spirit of oneness that should fill each soul with thanksgiving. In both these revealed prayers, the blessing that is identified for taking upon us His name, always remembering Him, and keeping His commandments is *that they* (us) *may always have his Spirit to be with them* (D&C 20:77).

If we take upon us His name, strive to remember Him, and keep His commandments, are we not disciples of Christ and are worthy to have His Spirit to be with us? The outcome of oneness is borne in the Savior's own modern-day witness.

> *And the Father and I are one. I am in the Father and the Father in me; and inasmuch as* **ye have received me, ye are in me and I in you** (D&C 50:43, emphasis added).

The scriptures provide valuable insight that to be one with Father and Christ we must be purified, we must be clean or the oneness relationship cannot take place. Purification comes through the blood of Christ, a result of the Atonement. No unclean thing can enter into Father's kingdom. This instruction was given by Christ to Father's children in the new world.

> *And* **no unclean thing can enter into his kingdom;** *therefore nothing entereth into his rest save it be those who have washed their garments in my blood, because of their faith, and the repentance of all their sins, and their faithfulness unto the end* (3 Nephi 27:19, emphasis added).

During Christ's visit to the people of Nephi assembled to receive His instruction, He went a small way off and offered prayer to Father for the twelve disciples He had called to lead the His church in the New World, providing this understanding.

Father, I thank thee that thou hast **purified** *those whom I have chosen, because of their faith, and I pray for them, and also for them who shall believe on their words, that they may be* **purified in me**, *through faith on their words,* **even as they are purified in me.**

Father, I pray not for the world, but for those whom thou hast given me out of the world, because of their faith, **that they may be purified in me, that I may be in them as thou, Father, art in me, that we may be one, that I may be glorified in them** (3 Nephi 19:28-29, emphasis added).

This principle of oneness is both wonderful and eternal. Father and Jesus Christ are one in purpose, vision, work, mission, instruction, and blessing. They are one in completing the "Plan of Salvation" for each of Father's children. Their work is to bring us together in the name of Christ **in one,** that we may be **one with Them**, requiring that we be purified. Our work is to assist. What a glorious opportunity. Loving them with all our souls and obeying Christ's commandments are two of the ways we can evidence our appreciation for this glorious blessing with a depth beyond temporal understanding.

CHAPTER 6

———⊸o𝒞𝒮ᴐo⊷———

DEEP AFFECTION FOR JESUS CHRIST

I f you had spent a great deal of time and energy in aligning yourself with the Master, following Jesus Christ as His disciple, how would you feel having your love for Him seemingly questioned? As we have already pondered, the likely outcome was to put Peter's love in perspective. Either way, that must have been an incredibly stressful experience for Simon Peter. However, the Savior had Peter's attention and this apostle proved his love from that moment on.

Peter's experience with the Lord mirrors our own as an example regarding being challenged and needing to consider our honest responses. Have we given ourselves to sacred counsel sufficiently to answer as Peter did? What are the similarities between Peter's confrontation and our own?

> *And Jesus, walking by the sea of Galilee, saw two brethren, Simon called Peter, and Andrew his brother, casting a net into the sea: for they were fishers.*
>
> *And he saith unto them, **Follow me, and I will make you fishers of men.***
>
> *And they straightway left their nets, and followed him* (Matthew 4:18-20, emphasis added).

36

Perhaps, this experience seems a little hard to believe. Can you imagine yourself being called in this fashion and responding as Peter and Andrew did? Have you been called by the Savior to bless the lives of others, called to make a difference in their lives?

> ***Therefore, hold up your light that it may shine unto the world. Behold I am the light which ye shall holdup—*** *that which ye have seen me do. Behold ye see that I have prayed unto the Father, and ye all have witnessed.*
>
> ***And ye see that I have commanded that none of you should go away, but rather have commanded that ye should come unto me, that ye might feel and see; even so shall ye do unto the world;*** *and whosoever breaketh this commandment suffereth himself to be led into temptation* (3 Nephi 18:24-25, emphasis added).

It is very clear that we all have been invited and a call awaits our response. We have been instructed to hold up our light unto the world and the Savior is that Light. This is a commandment. It is also a witness of our love for Him, our affection.

> *For the word of the Lord is truth, and whatsoever is truth is light, and whatsoever is light is Spirit, even the Spirit of Jesus Christ.*
>
> *And the Spirit giveth light to every man that cometh into the world, and the Spirit enlighteneth every man through the world, that hearkeneth to the voice of the Spirit.*
>
> *And every one that hearkeneth to the voice of the Spirit cometh unto God, even the Father* (D&C 84:45-47).

Truth is light. Light is Spirit, *even the Spirit of Jesus Christ.* This information is vital for all of God's children. How can they come to God without this instruction? Would holding up our Light (Jesus

Christ) also make us "fishers of men" within whatever call we receive?" Indeed, it would.

Peter and the other apostles were taught directly by Jesus Christ. We each have the "Light of Christ" given to us upon our entry into this mortal world and it will guide us, if we are listening, to truth, light, the Holy Ghost, and Jesus Christ. We are invited by Jesus Christ to receive the gift of the Holy Ghost, that we may be blessed even as Christ's original apostles were blessed. Invitation, instruction, and conversion are all components of the process of receiving and embracing truth. We are following the example of the apostles if we have accepted this call.

If the Savior, in a private moment with you alone, examined the "loves" you focus on right now, and asked, calling you by name, *Lovest thou me more than these?* What would be your answer? If you responded in the affirmative, what do you think He would instruct you to do regarding the exercise and application of that love? You know His instruction to Peter. Perhaps prayerful asking would prepare you with a soft, receptive heart and strong, faithful determination to receive what the Lord would have you know and do.

What if your answer is no or that you are not sure? Answering invites pondering and honesty. What areas of life are you most passionate about? What do they include? business, boating, golf, travel, cars, gardening, or any other possession or activity? Would you answer differently if you were standing in the presence of the Savior instead of kneeling by your bed at home?

The Savior's question to Peter about love and fish invites for us to focus on personal "loves". What if we have a love that would not be considered positive or constructive? There are people who seemingly love anger, raging against God for any challenge in life or anyone who has crossed their path and disagrees with them on something, sometimes anything. Some individuals find joy in demeaning and hurting others, finding pleasure in doing that which is destructive. Our loves can be positive or negative depending upon whether they are filled with truth and light, or they are not. However, true love is only positive, constructive, and is the love of and for Jesus Christ.

What about those "loves" that we don't recognize as loves? Have you made covenants in your membership of the Savior's church and the Kingdom of God? Have you made other promises? What if you haven't conscientiously attempted to keep them? This isn't about perfection, as none of us is perfect. This may be about promises that you gave yourself a "pass" on. They aren't "loves," but they don't measure up to your promise and ability. Think of movies and music, books and magazines. Does the content measure up to promises you made to God? What about profanity and taking the Lord's name in vain? Do you give yourself a pass at times when you are really angry, or some other emotion has you fired up?

As you ponder, are there little sins that you hate to give up, or don't seem very important. Can you say with an honest heart, "I am clean?" These things that our lives are filled with are the "fish" in this instruction of the Lord. How many times does He have to ask us if we love Him more than them? Knowing where your love, loyalties, and true desires are, is essential in aligning yourself with Christ. Loving Him is the grand key. Prayerful asking, listening, and patience throughout our lives are required to support us in that love and the fulfillment of the responsibilities He has given us.

The reality is that perfection will elude us in mortality. Do we excuse ourselves for the little sins we commit even though they will have a crippling effect on our progression along the covenant path by ignoring them, treating them as if they were "other loves?" Do we love the Savior more than these? He paid the price for forgiveness, but genuine repentance is required for this gift to be given and received.

> *Behold, he who has repented of his sins, the same is forgiven, and I, the Lord, remember them no more.*
>
> *By this ye may know if a man repenteth of his sins— behold, he will confess them and forsake them (D&C 58:42-43).*
>
> *Yea, and as often as my people repent will I forgive them their trespasses against me* (Mosiah 26:30).

Our Father loves each of His children and has given them gifts and opportunities for experiences that have the potential influence to make substantive differences in each child's life, as required in the preparation and worthiness to receive the gift of Eternal Life. The value of these gifts is beyond anything the world can give, or we can imagine. Without an overriding love for Jesus Christ, all the experience and gifts that remain with the individual have no power to qualify the person for the blessing of returning Home and the supreme gift of Eternal Life.

Jesus Christ was not just making helpful suggestions when he responded to the lawyer, who desired to tempt Him into saying something that could be used against Him. The lawyer asked,

> *Master, which is the great commandment in the law? Jesus said unto him, Thou shalt love the Lord thy God with all thy heart, and with all thy soul, and with all they mind. This is the first and great commandment* (Matthew 22:36- 38).

The commandment, second only to the first, is *Thou shalt love thy neighbour as thyself* (Matthew 22:39). To love according to the first and second commandments is to love as Jesus Christ loves.

Loving the Savior with all our heart, mind, and soul supersedes all other loves and interests. The additional miracle that some might not expect is that if we love the Savior more than anything else, all other of our loves, interests, and affections will be aligned in our lives to provide the greatest blessing.

The supernal gift of Eternal Life and the requirement essential for receipt, love for God, is so evident in many of the recorded instructions from Jesus Christ. In fact, it appears that learning to love and making love the energy and focus of your life is the foundation of life here and life eternal. All of God's commandments are given with the foundational requirement that obedience must be accompanied and powered by love.

For whosoever will save his life, must be willing to lose it for my sake; and whosoever will be willing to lose his life for my sake, the same shall save it.

For what doth it profit a man if he gain the whole world, and yet he receive him not who God hath ordained, and he lose his own soul, and he himself be a castaway (JST Luke 9:24-25, Joseph Smith's translation)?

He that loveth father or mother more than me is not worthy of me: and he that loveth son or daughter more than me is not worthy of me (Matthew 10:37).

A new commandment I give unto you, That ye love one another; as I have loved you, that ye also love one another.

By this shall all men know that ye are my disciples, if ye have love one to another (John 13:34- 35).

Do these quotes stir your soul, prompting the desire for understanding and confirmation as truth? The way has been provided for any of God's children to receive validation that the instruction given by Jesus Christ, His apostles, or any of God's children who follow Christ as disciples and is confirmed by the Spirit is correct. Confirmation comes by the whisperings of the Spirit to the person whose heart is soft enough to receive. Christ gave this instruction to His apostles.

But the Comforter, which is the Holy Ghost, whom the Father will send in my name, he shall teach you all things, and bring all things to your remembrance, whatsoever I have said unto you (John 14:26).

Instruction. Remembering. It is vitally important to know that it is the Holy Ghost's mission to teach and confirm all things that are required for us to return Home and be worthy to receive the gift of Eternal Life.

The Spirit itself beareth witness with our spirit, that we are the children of God:

And if children, then heirs; heirs of God, and joint-heirs with Christ; if so be that we suffer with him, that we may be also glorified together (Romans 8:16-17).

The Apostle Paul in this letter to the Roman saints, bore witness that we are the children of God and joint heirs with Jesus Christ. Fulfilling the requirements of being an heir qualifies us to receive all the blessings God has for His children. It is vital for us to **remember** that we are heirs, inheritors with Jesus Christ. We are not alone, but we must accept responsibility as Christ has, for the receipt of God's gifts and for their use.

To *suffer with Him* is to align our desires and lives with Him, including outcomes. We must be willing to *suffer* persecution, and any other requirement made of us to continue as heirs and receive Father's blessings. Can you imagine doing this without loving Him?

Carefully read and embrace the depth and breadth of the Holy Ghost's responsibilities to you as a child of God and as an heir, as revealed in these scriptures.

For what man knoweth the things of a man, save the spirit of man which is in him? Even so the things of God knoweth no man, but the Spirit of God.

Now we have received, not the spirit of the world, but the spirit which is of God; that we might know the things that are freely given to us of God.

Which things also we speak, not in the words which man's wisdom teacheth, but which the Holy Ghost teacheth; comparing spiritual things with spiritual (1 Corinthians 2:11-13).

Angels speak by the power of the Holy Ghost; wherefore they speak the words of Christ. Wherefore, I said unto you, feast upon the words of Christ; for behold, the words of Christ will tell you all things what ye should do (2 Nephi 32:3).

This instruction from the Apostle Paul and Nephi makes it very clear regarding the Holy Ghost's teaching and confirming ministrations to the children of God, if the children are willing to receive. Through the Holy Ghost we can learn and embrace the *words of Christ* and in doing so we will be told all that we should do as Nephi testified. As an heir and as a disciple of Christ, doesn't this promise fill your soul with thanksgiving for God's love and care?

If you are uncertain about God's promises and your relationship with Jesus Christ, this instruction from the prophet Moroni provides the truth and light (D&C 84:45, 93:36) needed to genuinely inquire of Father regarding the promises made.

> *And when ye shall receive these things, I would exhort you that ye would ask God, the Eternal Father, in the name of Christ, if these things are not true; and if ye shall ask with a sincere heart, with real intent, having faith in Christ, he will manifest the truth of it unto you, by the power of the Holy Ghost.*
>
> *And by the power of the Holy Ghost ye may know the truth of all things.*
>
> *And whatsoever thing is good is just and true; wherefore, nothing that is good denieth the Christ, but acknowledgeth that he is.*
>
> *And ye may know that he is, by the power of the Holy Ghost; wherefore I would exhort you that ye deny not the power of God; for he worketh by power, according to the faith of the children of men, the same today and tomorrow, and forever* (Moroni 10:4-7).

In common language, love has this definition: a strong feeling of warm personal attachment or deep affection, such as for a parent or child (dictionary.com). Do you have a deep affection for Jesus Christ. Can your relationship with Him be described as a "warm personal attachment?" If not, this does not change His love or desire and will for you. These scriptures and others await your review and acceptance, trusting God to assist and fill your soul with truth and light, leading to love and a "deep affection" for Christ and Father.

> *For you shall live by every word that proceedeth forth from the mouth of God.*
>
> *For the word of the Lord is truth, and whatsoever is truth is light, and whatsoever is light is Spirit, even the Spirit of Jesus Christ.*
>
> *And the Spirit giveth light to every man that cometh into the world; and the Spirit enlighteneth every man through the world, that hearkeneth to the voice of the Spirit.*
>
> *And everyone that hearkenth to the voice of the Spirit cometh unto God, even the Father* (D&C 84:44-47).

It should be obvious that not all the passions, desires, and attitudes God's children may possess are components or outcomes of love. Those that are not may have their origins in greed, selfishness, pride, envy, hate, and immorality to name a few. True love has none of these. Therefore, it is easy to understand why the Apostle John said,

> *Beloved, let us love one another: for love is of God; and every one that loveth is born of God, and knoweth God.*
>
> *He that loveth not knoweth not God* (1 John 4:7-8).

True love, pure love, originates from Jesus Christ and our Father. There is no other original source.

> *As the Father hath loved me, so have I loved you: continue ye in my love.*
>
> *If ye keep my commandments, ye shall abide in my love; even as I have kept my Father's commandments, and abide in his love.*
>
> *These things have I spoken unto you, that my joy might remain in you, and that your joy might be full.*

This is my commandment, That ye love one another, as I have loved you (John 15:9-12).

We exercise and prove our love for the Savior when we receive His love and affirm our love for Him by keeping His commandments. True love is fulfilled when it is received with thanksgiving and given to others freely, without obligation. It is easy to love those who love us. It approaches being "godlike" when we love those who don't love us or have any relationship with us. Love is a gift that we can give everyone and should give. We are all Father's children. We are all members of the same family. Love is a family component and of Godhood.

CHAPTER 7

—◦◦◦◦◦—

THE PURE LOVE OF CHRIST

And hereby we do know that we know him, if we keep his commandments.

He that saith, I know him, and keepeth not his commandments, is a liar, and the truth is not in him.

But whoso keepeth his word, in him verily is the love of God perfected: hereby know we that we are in him (1 John 2:3-5).

The love of God is perfected or becomes complete when we keep His word, obeying His commandments. Love invites companionship, kindness, caring, loyalty, service, sacrifice, as well as obedience, all the attributes that bring us together, facilitating the receipt of joy. Love causes us to focus outward on others, anxious for their comfort and welfare, that being more important than our own, which is an inward focus.

The prophet Moroni received a personal ministration from Christ. In response to the Savior's instruction Moroni replied in this way about the Savior's love.

And now I know that this love which thou hast had for the children of men is charity; wherefore, except men shall have charity they cannot inherit that place which thou hast prepared in the mansions of thy Father (Ether 12:34).

It is essential for all of Father's children to understand the Savior's love, which is identified as charity. Charity is more inclusive than love, as we know it temporally. It is of a higher order, being stronger and more noble, centered on virtue, delights in blessing others, and is eternal in nature. Father's children can progress and be gifted with charity, filling their souls, which each of us is required to receive and embrace, in order to become as Christ is.

> *Wherefore, my beloved brethren, pray unto the Father with all the energy of heart, that ye may be filled with this love, which he hath bestowed upon all who are true followers of his Son, Jesus Christ; that ye may become the sons of God; that when he shall appear we shall be like him, for we shall see him as he is; that we may have this hope; that we may be purified even as he is pure. Amen* (Moroni 7:48).

Moroni's prayerful testimony on behalf of all of Father's children should resonate with our souls and enrich our understanding sufficiently that we commit to do as he advises as a way of life, that we become true followers. The instructions are so plain and clear. We cannot become a true disciple of Christ without being filled with this love, with charity. Our worthiness to return Home is conditioned upon it. Charity actuates the aligning of our lives with Christ, the energizing and refining power needed to prepare us to be worthy to be in His presence.

> *. . . if a man be meek and lowly in heart, and confesses by the power of the Holy Ghost that Jesus is the Christ, he must needs have charity; for if he have not charity he is nothing; wherefore he must needs have charity.*
>
> *But charity is the pure love of Christ, and it endureth forever; and whoso is found possessed of it at the last day, it shall be well with him* (Moroni 7:44, 47).

Are there different kinds or qualities of love, aside from charity? The answer is yes. When love is defined as "deep affection," we can exercise that quality in our lives for many things: objects, people, ideas, attitudes; there are many options.

When love is defined as charity, it is separated from all other expressions of love. It is vital that we remember that we must be *meek and lowly in heart* and confess *by the power of the Holy Ghost that Jesus is the Christ.* If we do not, we have not charity and we are as the scripture says, *nothing.*

Is it enough to say, I am filled with "the pure love of Christ" or I am filled with charity? What testimonies of love do the decisions and efforts of our lives bear? It is clear that we must progress in seeking, embracing, and exercising love in order to love as the Savior loves.

> *In this was manifested the love of God toward us, because that God sent his only begotten Son into the world, that we might live through him.* (1 John 4:9).

Christ's life bears witness of is His charity and is exemplified without equal in the performance of the Atonement. This act provides for repentance and the filling of all requirements needed to return Home and be in Christ's and Father's presence.

CHAPTER 8

———◇○◇○◇———

DRAWING NEARER TO THE SAVIOR

In the visitation from Jesus Christ discussed earlier, Moroni also made this comment:

> *And again, I remember that thou hast said that thou hast loved the world, even unto the laying down of thy life for the world, that thou mightiest take it again to prepare a place for the children of men* (Ether 12:33).

The Savior loves the world or all of Father's children so deeply that He was willing to lay His mortal life down, perform the Atonement, and to pick His life up again to provide the blessings needed by all to prepare the way for our return Home. He met all requirements of the Atonement, and now we have the opportunity through the Savior's love and sacrifice to partner with Him in putting our lives in order and becoming worthy to be in Father's presence. Is the love expended for our salvation even comprehensible to us? Yet, it is real, and our souls recognize it if we turn to the source of all truth and light, Jesus Christ. Read His words and feel the love.

Draw near unto me and I will draw near unto you; seek me diligently and ye shall find me; ask, and ye shall receive; knock, and it shall be opened unto you (D&C 88:63).

We have been instructed to "draw" near unto the Savior. Can that even happen if we don't love Him in return as deeply and profoundly as we can? Giving this kind of love is no small thing.

If ye love me, keep my commandments (John 14:15).

He that hath my commandments, and keepeth them, he it is that loveth me: and he that loveth me shall be loved of my Father, and I will love him, and will manifest myself to him (John 14:21).

Keeping His commandments should be the first and most basic of our desires and attempts to learn to love as Christ loves and draw nearer to Him. Loyalty, even in its beginning stages, is important in building relations that have even temporal value, is essential in building relationships with the power to last beyond time and distance.

Consider this—what would you think or how would you feel if in a moment of quiet reflection, while you are trying to find your way with a challenging problem, you heard in your heart and mind together, *don't you trust Me to get you where you need to be*? Would this inquiry deserve some intense, deeply personal evaluation for an answer? Would your exercise of faith and prayer change in seeking an answer, increasing your understanding? This question is essential in our lives no matter how it is asked. How we answer is vital to our salvation.

The challenge of giving trust to God and exercising sufficient faith that His will is in the process of being fulfilled by us, perhaps not all at once and certainly not perfectly, but is progressing as we develop spiritually. This is a challenge that all of us can meet. It requires constant striving, listening to the Spirit, and aligning our lives with God's will through our obedience and exercise of love. This has been experienced by all of Father's children throughout history. It is part of the mortal experience of turning to the Savior and meeting the challenge of continuous exercise of faith, trusting that all will be done according to His will. Very often, patience is required—a trait that many of us are still trying to master, but essential.

Consider King Limhi, whose people were in bondage to the Lamanites, suffering the experiences that captivity and oppression bring. This was the king's instruction to them on the eve of deliverance.

> *Therefore, lift up your heads, and rejoice, and **put your trust in God**, in that God who was the God of Abraham, and Isaac, and Jacob; and also, that God who brought the children of Israel out of the land of Egypt, and caused that they should walk through the Red Sea on dry ground, and fed them with manna that they might not perish in the wilderness; and many more things did he do for them* (Mosiah 7:19, emphasis added).

How vital it is in building our trust in God to remember, to remember His power and blessing to others. This answers the unspoken question, since He can do those things for others, can't He do the same for us?

Another important example is Mormon's (the prophet/compiler of the Book of Mormon) comment regarding Alma and his people who were about to be put in bondage to the Lamanites.

> *Nevertheless the Lord seeth fit to chasten his people; yea, he trieth their patience and their faith.*
>
> *Nevertheless—**whosoever putteth his trust** in him the same shall be lifted up at the last day. Yea, and thus it was with this people* (Mosiah 23:21-22, emphasis added).

The Lord determined to discipline His people by trying their patience and faith. The remedy, the resolve for what was to come was for these people to begin to trust the Lord. Can it be any different in our day?

King Mosiah, speaking to his people about his proposed change in their government from having a king to rule by judges, made this inciteful comment, thinking about King Limhi's people, their bondage and being made free.

> *But behold, he* (the Lord) *did deliver them because they did humble themselves before him; and because they cried mightily unto him he did deliver them out of bondage; and thus doth the Lord work with his power in all cases among the children of men, extending the arm of mercy towards them that* **put their trust in him** (Mosiah 29:20, emphasis added).

These scriptural witnesses bear powerful testimony of the Lord's requirements to intervene in His children's life challenges and to provide blessings that can only be given by the exercise of trust in His love and care. Our relationship with the Lord is ultimately built upon trust, which requires the exercise of faith, hope, patience, and love.

It is important to understand that if we truly love Him, we will naturally strive to keep His commandments, and this effort will fill our souls with indescribable happiness. That is the promise King Benjamin, the prophet/king in the Book of Mormon described perfectly in speaking to his people.

> *And moreover, I would desire that y should consider on the blessed and happy state of those that keep the commandments of God. For behold, they are blessed in all things, both temporal and spiritual; and if they hold out faithful to the end they are received into heaven, that thereby they may dwell with God in a state of never-ending happiness. O remember, remember that these things are true; for the Lord God hath spoken it* (Mosiah 2:41).

One of the consequences that occurs as we make our way through mortality, perhaps unintended by us, is that we will bear testimony, or lack thereof, of Him and our love continually through our thoughts, actions, and desires. To add to the depth of that happiness described by King Benjamin, we must embrace the knowledge that we will also be loved of the Father, and Christ will manifest Himself to us if we truly love Him (John 14:21). Would those blessings transform you?

> *And now I know that this love which thou hast had for the children of men is charity; wherefore, except men shall have charity they cannot inherit that place which thou hast prepared in the mansions of thy Father* (Ether 12:34).

Moroni has given us an enhanced understanding of the Savior's love. He has also confirmed for us that it is Christ's desire that we grow, mature, and progress sufficiently to be filled with this love.

> *Draw near unto me and I will draw near unto you . . .* (D&C 88:63).

We examined this instruction of the Savior near the beginning of this discussion. Now, with contributions of additional scriptures, Christ's promise to draw near to you as you strive to get closer to Him witnesses on a very personal level His love for you, for all of Father's children. The richness of the spiritual record testifies boldly and powerfully of this love.

John, the Savior's apostle, bore witness that we can come to know Christ and have our love for Him "perfected," meaning improved or refined.

> *And hereby we do know that we know him, if we keep his commandments.*
>
> *He that saith, I know him, and keepeth not his commandments, is a liar, and the truth is not in him.*
>
> *But whoso keepeth his word, in him verily is the love of God perfected . . .* (1 John 2:3-5).

If we keep His commandments, not only will our love be "perfected," but by doing so, we will come to know Him. Is this one of your desires? The answer to do so is simple. Keep His commandments. Love will enlighten and align your efforts with Him.

Pure love. Perfect love. What is pure or perfect love? Do we use the term love often or too loosely to describe our feelings about something? Is what we are feeling not really love, but an attraction, something that stirs our emotions, bringing us comfort or excitement? But is that really love? Perhaps not.

We know the Savior is perfect, so His love is perfect. As we examine His life, we are able to witness the actions and interactions of perfect love: kindness, caring, sacrifice, loyalty to Father, obedience, joy, sorrow for the sins of the world, prayer, courage, understanding, witness of truth, patience, lifting of burdens, healings, companionship, peace-giving, forgiving, empathy, sympathy, long-suffering, truthfulness, and selflessness. This is not a complete list, as you might have anticipated, but it does illustrate the breadth of Christ's love.

Can we love Christ perfectly? Not right now, not here is this fallen world, but that day can and will come depending upon our desires, decisions, and effort to be His true disciple. However, the more we emulate His example, the more we exercise our love as He does, we will be permitted to draw closer to Him, to assist in His work, all of which will have a refining effect upon our souls.

For behold, this is my work and my glory—to bring to pass the immortality and eternal life of man (Mose 1:39).

To exercise love as Christ loves, to have our minds and hearts united with the attitudes that invite truth and light into our lives, we must become like children.

*But Jesus called them unto him, and said, Suffer little **children** to come unto me, and forbid them not: for of such is the kingdom of God.*

*Verily I say unto you, Whosoever shall not receive the kingdom of God as **a little child** shall in no wise enter therein* (Luke 18:16-17, emphasis added).

Ye have heard that it hath been said, Thou shalt love thy neighbour, and hate thine enemy.

*But I say unto you, **Love** your enemies, bless them that curse you, do good to them that hate you, and pray for them which despitefully use you, and persecute you;*

*That ye may be the **children** of your Father which is in heaven: for he maketh his sun to rise on the evil and on the good, and sendeth rain on the just and on the unjust* (Matthew 5:43-45, emphasis added).

CHAPTER 9

⋙∘ᴄ⟆⟑∘⋘

BECOMETH AS A CHILD

Jesus Christ has made it perfectly clear that in order for God's children, for us, to be worthy to return Home and be with Him, we must become as children. So, that raises the question, what is it about children that we must emulate, embrace, and make it part of who we are?

King Benjamin, in a major address to his people, gave this instruction, which helps answer the question before us.

> *For the natural man is an enemy to God, and has been from the fall of Adam, and will be forever and ever, unless he yields to the enticings of the Holy Spirit, and putteth off the natural man and becometh a saint through the atonement of Christ the Lord, and* ***becometh as a child, submissive, meek, humble, patient, full of love, willing to submit to all things which the Lord seeth fit to inflict upon him, even as a child doth submit to his father*** *(Mosiah 3:19, emphasis added).*

Thankfully, this prophet king, after having visited with an angel, gave this instruction that details the qualities that each of us must strive for to become as children and be worthy and prepared to return Home and be in Father's presence.

> But the **natural man** receiveth not the things of the Spirit of God: for they are foolishness unto him: neither can he know them, because they are spiritually discerned (1 Corinthians 2:14, emphasis added).
>
> . . . and the wise and the learned, and they that are rich, who are puffed up because of their learning, and their wisdom, and their riches—yea, they are they whom he despiseth (2 Nephi 9:42).

The "natural man" is he or she that will not humble themselves and turn to God seeking repentance and the blessings of the Spirit. Being wise, learned, and rich are attributes that do not disqualify a person from becoming a saint. However, when combined with pride or being puffed up and doing dishonorable things, God despises those conditions, and they disqualify that person unless there is repentance and a change of effort and life. The remedy is to *becometh as a child* with the qualities that accompany one in being a child, anxious to progress and to do those things that please God, even as children desire to please their parents.

The sons of Mosiah and the brethren that accompanied them on their mission to the Lamanites met together near the end of their mission and were discussing the wonders and blessings bestowed by God on the converts and themselves. After rehearsing what they had witnessed of the Lord's mercies and the conversion that took place, Ammon said,

> And now behold, my brethren, what **natural man** is there that knoweth these things? I say unto you, there is none that knoweth these things, save it be the penitent (Alma 26:21, emphasis added).

Knowing what the natural man or woman is, we can readily begin to understand that the counsel in Mosiah 3:19 of the Book of Mormon was given to help each of us to change our identity to become a disciple of Jesus Christ and to do so requires repentance, faithfulness and becoming like a child.

This doctrine is taught in many different forms in our Sunday worship experiences as we sit with adults and children alike. We find it in the scriptures, lesson manuals, and the shared experiences of teachers and students. How many times have you reread a scripture only to find in a later reading something has changed? As you ponder upon it, you discover that it is you that has changed, not the scriptures. Now, what you have read is no longer just an interesting thought. Now you feel it, comprehending it in greater detail and increased clarity.

Perhaps you recall Nephi's pointed explanation to his brothers as their murmurings boarded on rebellion regarding the Lord's commandment to build a ship and other instructions in the land they called Bountiful.

> *Ye are swift to do iniquity but slow to remember the Lord your God. Ye have seen an angel, and he spake unto you; yea, ye have heard his voice from time to time; and he hath spoken unto you in a still small voice, but ye were past feeling, that ye could not **feel his words** . . .* (1 Nephi 17:45, emphasis added).

Hearing or receiving is important, but does not guarantee understanding. Feeling requires a depth of recognition, understanding, and acceptance at the core of the soul, providing increased comprehension.

Since "feeling" is so important in comprehending spiritual instruction and impressions, how does spiritual feeling differ from the other feelings we have as mortals throughout our lives? How do we tell the difference? Think about all the feelings you have had in your life. Are they all spiritual and inspirational? Are they mixed with more worldly feelings or can you tell?

Consider this list as the items relate to your ponderings: love, hate, happy, sad, angry, depressed, joyful, funny, fun, sympathy, empathy, hungry, thirsty, concern, shame, sorrow, hopeful, sorry, pained, trusting, tired, energized, sleepy, believing, suspicious, despairing, prideful, judgmental, selfish, disappointed, and likely many more.

With so many feelings that are part of our lives, how do we discern those that are just a part of mortality from those that are inspirational, answers from Heaven according to our prayers and needs? Many are capable of obscuring objectivity. The need is real to distance ourselves from those feelings that don't permit us to see and feel differently as needed; to feel closer to God, to desire to be faithful children, to obey and lift the burdens of others having a sincere desire to draw even nearer to them.

We must turn away from those feelings that seem to distract us from drawing nearer and increase the thoughts that are selfish and banish them from our souls, choosing that which is of light from that which is born of darkness.

Those feelings that are positive, that invite peace, love, awakening, the lifting of our spirit, filling us with a desire to be faithful to God and align our lives with His will through repentance, humility, meekness, and serving others, these are feelings that will lead us to finding joy in righteousness and inspiration in our ponderings and prayers.

God, in His great love for His children, sent an angel to King Benjamin, with instruction that was to be delivered to his people regarding the coming and mission of His Only Begotten Son. Consider for a moment (and longer) how benevolent God is, how important this message was and is, and the necessity for clarity to dispatch an angel.

The messenger bore witness of the coming of the Savior, Jesus Christ, and that God's salvation for His children comes only through the name, power, and mission of His First Born, the Lord Omnipotent. King Benjamin's entire discourse deserves to be read and reread, chapters 2-4 in Mosiah in the Book of Mormon. The blessings that follow for your benefit may be as if you had been in that original congregation.

King Benjamin spoke forcefully that *men drink damnation to their own souls except they humble themselves and become as little children* (Mosiah 3:18). In verse 19 he gave this profound instruction that we must yield to the *enticings* of the Holy Spirit, put off the *natural man*, and become a *saint through the atonement of Christ the Lord.*

In that same verse, he then instructs on how this is done as recorded above—by **becoming as a child,** *submissive, meek, humble, patient, full of love, willing to submit to all things which the Lord seeth fit to inflict upon him, even as a child doth submit to his father.* These six required actions are actually childlike qualities of character that precipitate the resultant actions and desired outcomes: Jesus Christ being the perfect example of their application and use. They help to answer the question of how we can tell the difference between mortal/worldly and spiritual feelings, those that have refining and purifying properties.

These traits are all necessary to the progression process needed for each of God's children at any time, without discrimination of ability, age, race, culture, experience, sins, or personal goals. The need or requirement is global and yet so personal for you, for me, for everyone. They are given as divine gifts requiring the desire to use and the exercise of faith, prayer, and effort. These qualities are much more than knowledge, as important as knowledge is. They initiate divine, service-inspired actions when desire is felt by the heart and deep within our soul.

The prophet Nephi explained how this is confirmed by the Spirit within the heart . . . *the power of the Holy Ghost carrieth it unto the hearts of the children of men* (2 Nephi 33:1). The Holy Ghost will deliver the message with divine clarity of truth. However, if our hearts are not soft enough, we may not "feel" the message, being left without the witness of God's instruction and love. This is a tragedy that can be reversed by seeking these childlike qualities of character.

How soft is your heart? Are you willing to receive correction, instruction, and course alignment as needed? Are you willing to commit to the journey to move forward from worldly experience, the application of adult maturity (sometimes questionable), and the perceptions of power, influence, and achievement to make it all subservient to progression in **becoming as a child**? That question may test our trust in God.

In one of the Savior's teaching experiences with the people in His homeland, they brought their infants to Him, hoping He would touch them. The scripture says the disciples rebuked the people for doing this. However, the Savior said,

> . . . *Suffer little children to come unto me, and forbid them not: for of such is the kingdom of God.*
> *Verily I say unto you, Whosoever shall not receive the kingdom of God as a little child shall in no wise enter therein* (Luke 18:16-17).

We must become childlike, anxiously seeking alignment with Christ while we learn to cherish divine influence through gaining simple understanding, trust, and exercising humble faith to produce innocence and purity. Hearing and feeling, the awakening that brings understanding is delivered by the Spirit with divine power and sensitivity.

God speaks through inspiration and scripture in terms of family with powerful invitation to accept and recognize Him as our literal parent, our Father, the Father of our spirits. His desire for us? mortal experience within a divine family influence, educating and preparing us for a return Home. Even in that sacred place our progression must continue for us to become "complete" or perfect and worthy of Life Eternal.

Give your loyalty to Father and His Only Begotten Son, whose "work and glory" are *to bring to pass the immortality and eternal life of man* (Moses 1:39), of His children, of you.

CHAPTER 10

❧◦❀◦❧

BEING SUBMISSIVE

. . . becometh as a child, **submissive** *. . .* (Mosiah 3:19, emphasis added).

Two of the synonyms of submissive are compliant and obedient. Being submissive is a choice even with children. Parents rejoice in the days that come when a young child begins to make the decisions necessary for obedience, when self-control and understanding transform disobedience into obedience.

My wife, Jerry, had a wonderful teaching moment with one of our children that encouraged early in life the making of choices to be submissive to mother's instruction is the right decision. This child was classified in the "terrible twos." Each day our children, a daughter and son, sat at the bar in the kitchen for lunch. Jerry would pour milk in a small glass for each child and invariably our son would spill it. She would clean it up, pour another glass and give instruction on how to handle the drink. It became obvious that this exercise on his part was intentional, perhaps it was fun. What power there is in simple acts, controlling the actions of others.

One day, when Jerry decided this ritual must come to an end and after another spilling episode, she acted using a different teaching technique. The milk was spilled. She cleaned it up as expected. Our son must have quietly enjoyed this power play. Another glass was poured, a pause followed, and then the milk was thrown in the child's face. After cleaning him and the kitchen up, a wise decision was made by one so young—he never spilled it again on purpose. He was a child and submitted to his mother's will.

Motivation is a part of mortality. When hungry, people look for food. When sleepy, it's time for rest. Those decisions seem quite easy for fulfillment to be provided. Every person has a range of motivators. Some are healthy, having intrinsic value and others can be labeled "empty temptations" as they have no potential for sustenance or real value to body or spirit. The same is true with motivators and aligning our lives with Christ.

Those that have actual recognized value are the principles and attributes that are worthy of submitting ourselves to. What personal principles, ideas, and considerations ought to be placed on a list for you? Perhaps examining your considerations by this worldly standard might be helpful, **What's in it for me?** Honest evaluation assisted by the Light of Christ (our conscience) and the Holy Ghost will bring clarity to your understanding and decision-making.

Submitting invites change. It can be positive or negative depending on what we submit to and how much we give of ourselves to it. If we submit to anger, can it give us anything different than what it is? Is this the same for immorality? When people you know gave themselves to these and similar values, did they receive anything of redeeming worth from them?

People can turn from these by submitting to principles that are filled with light and positive potential. Appreciation of value comes in recognizing the contrast when light shines on the harmful and the good. Hate and love. Which will bless? Which will curse?

We can't avoid submitting. Decisions will be made regarding the temptations and influences in your life. Remember, doing nothing is a decision. Outcomes may not be within your vision, preventing you from deciding how it will turn out. Yet, choices will be made. Recognizing the influencers that are God's desires for us will make all the difference in our lives. They may not be the easiest, probably not as the world might view it. They will be the ones that refine your soul preparing you for blessings Father has in reserve, awaiting your progression and worthiness to receive.

The disciple James, who is reputed to be the Savior's brother, offered this succinct counsel.

> *Submit yourselves therefore to God. Resist the devil, and he will flee from you.*
> *Draw nigh unto God, and he will draw nigh to you* (James 4:7-8).

This counsel is simple, yet incredibly beneficial and filled with the light to sanctify our souls. Are you willing to submit with the simple faith and trust so evident in children?

We can submit to our physical drives, attitudes, nature, and other people. Choosing not to be submissive to the weather, but choosing to be submissive to the desire to stay dry, such as using an umbrella when it rains, is an obvious option. There are always options leading to our health and progression. Perhaps the lowest form of submissiveness is giving in to a temptation, something that has no potential for being a blessing. The highest form is turning to God with full purpose of heart, yielding our hearts, our desires, and expending our efforts to be faithful unto Him.

Even those negative and destructive experiences can be turned around if we submit to God's will, repent, and learn from the experience. In fact, repentance is probably the common and necessary companion to submission. We must embrace them together.

Willingness to change, to submit, to prove out Godly instruction often rises from the ashes or unfertile ground of sin and the adversary's efforts to thwart our progress and divert our course. Submitting to God is an attitude and act that can only change and strengthen our souls as we repent of the poor choices we've made. Being submissive to truth and light is foundational to righteousness. What a wonderful place we would be in if we could say with the exercise of faith and honesty, "I am striving at all times to be a faithful child and do the will of Father."

Submitting is something each of us does throughout our lives in ways we may not even recognize. We submit to the laws of the land, nature and all its components, to physical, mental, and emotional challenges, to the processes required for an education, and probably many hundreds of other factors that impact our lives. Why then, do we push back on Christ's desires to instruct, guide, and propel us forward to becoming like Him? We have been given our agency to choose. Even so, there must be opposition in all things, so that choices can and must be made. We can't progress without making them.

For it must needs be, that there is an opposition in all things. If not so, my firstborn in the wilderness, righteousness could not be brought to pass, neither wickedness, neither holiness nor misery, neither good nor bad (2 Nephi 2:11).

In pondering upon this instruction from Lehi to his son, Jacob, we realize that agency and making choices are essential to who we are and certainly to our journey here in mortality. Why is it so hard at times to trust God and gain experience that will change our lives by making choices that will bless us? Yes, Satan does make imitations that may be inviting, but the promise of understanding and protection through the Light of Christ and the Gift of the Holy Ghost is real, and produce the outcomes that bless our lives.

We must remember that Satan and his followers are avowed enemies of God and those who are faithful. They employ "weapons" that have been refined and used for thousands of years in this war against righteousness. They know how to use our weaknesses against us and proffer temptations in a way that we may not recognize upfront how subversive these are. The "opposition" plays to carnal desires and attempts to use our weaknesses against us.

Therein is the challenge that often arises when we are preparing to submit to Father's will. We must not submit to unrighteousness.

Jesus Christ is the supreme example of being submissive. He who could have called forth a legion of angels for support, gave himself to the unjust decisions of Caiaphas, the high priest, and Pilot, Roman Prefect of Judea. He accepted the cup (submitted) Father had given Him to suffer for the blessing of all and complete the requirements of the Atonement.

> *Therefore I command you to repent—repent, lest I smite you by the rod of my mouth, and by my wrath, and by my anger, and your sufferings be sore—how sore you know not, how exquisite you know not, yea, how hard to bear you know not.*
>
> ***For behold, I, God, have suffered these things for all,*** *that they might not suffer if they would repent;*
>
> *But if they would not repent they must suffer even as I;*
>
> *Which suffering caused myself, even God, the greatest of all, to tremble because of pain, and to bleed at every pore, and to suffer both body and spirit—and would that I might not drink the bitter cup, and shrink—*
>
> *Nevertheless, glory be to the Father, and **I partook and finished my preparations** unto the children of men* (D&C 19:15-19, emphasis added).
>
> *And behold, I am the light and the life of the world; and I have drunk out of that bitter cup which the Father hath given me, and have glorified the Father in taking upon me the sins of the world, in the which **I have suffered the will of the father in all things from the beginning*** (3 Nephi 11:11, emphasis added).

If He, "the greatest of all," submitted to Father's will for the blessing of Father's family, are we not under the same responsibility for our families and ourselves? Jesus Christ is the source of those truths and the light that accompanies them.

CHAPTER 11

⋙○⟋⟍○⋘

BEING MEEK

*... becometh as a child, submissive, **meek** ...* (Mosiah 3:19, emphasis added).

"Meek" is such an interesting adverb or description. The definitions of the word according to the Merriam Webster online dictionary are as follows.

- Enduring injury with patience and without resentment. (Mild)
- Deficient in spirit and courage. (Submissive)
- Not violent or strong. (Modcratc)

After all the world has to say, the standard, the definition, the understanding of meek was established by the Savior Himself, He being the perfect example. In comparing the Savior's actions and life with these definitions, we can clearly see that in being meek as Jesus Christ was, these definitions are insufficient to describe Him.

- Christ did endure injury with patience and without resentment.
- He was not deficient in spirit and courage but chose to be submissive to accomplish Father's will and the blessing of our lives. This required strength of spirit and capacity beyond mortal ability.
- The Savior was not violent in His response to crucifixion, but to say He was not strong is totally incorrect. He endured suffering in completing the Atonement, including the part that

crucifixion played, the combined pain of which no person on earth has experienced.

Christ's actions define and illustrate the perfect example of meek and its application in our lives: patience without resentment even with personal injury and when things don't go as we planned; courage to be totally submissive to Father's will, trusting Him to guide us; enduring our challenges with patience and courage, the melding of those two qualities for our blessing. Consider these additional definitions: quiet, gentle, down-to-earth, modest, and unpretentious. Isn't Jesus Christ the ultimate example of these, all meanings being embodied in the word meek?

> *Take my yoke upon you, and learn of me; **for I am meek** and lowly in heart: and ye shall find rest unto your souls* (Matthew 11:29, emphasis added).

This statement of the Savior's clearly identifies how important being meek is. We are instructed to take upon us His yoke, effectively being joined together to live and labor similarly in spirit and manner according to His example. We become partners in His work. This very labor has the power to elevate our abilities and transform our souls to be worthy of sanctification—the very personal quality needed to return Home. We can't do it alone, but yoked with Him, all things can and will be done.

"Lowly in heart" is an interesting characterization used with meek. It suggests that our hearts are approachable, humble, soft, and willing, even anxious to make changes to align ourselves with God's desires.

It is worth noting that the summation of the various worldly definitions of meek suggests only being submissive or obedient, but do not address the natural outcome or gift of power that comes with the quality of being meek. Meekness is not disabling, but rather enabling, providing strength and ability; the two components of power to be used as directed by the Spirit and in our efforts to do good. Do not forget the promised outcome to *find rest unto your souls,* a gift beyond compare.

If someone labeled you in your teenage years as meek, how would you have felt about it? What about now? Is being meek a credit to you or a description of weakness? Submissive, humble, and patient are synonyms for meek and all share qualities of each other, but with their own unique focus. The world doesn't readily teach or encourage becoming meek. In fact, the spirit of the world seems to inspire and value pride, anger, and selfishness in a myriad of different ways. All are in opposition to developing the quality of meekness, some so subtle they may seem focused on that which is good, depending on the characteristics in how it is viewed, but join in concert with those ways that are an outright assault on Godly attitudes and actions.

The conversion of the sons of King Mosiah, as recorded in the Book of Mormon, provides a wonderful example of the necessity of becoming meek to receive all the blessings Father has for His children. In this example, the price the sons were required to pay for their rebellion becomes very clear and instructive for all those who read and ponder these scriptures. Defiance was ultimately replaced by meekness. Each son endeavored to align his life with his father's desires, and Heavenly Father's will. Without becoming meek, it could not have been done.

> *Now the sons of Mosiah were numbered among the unbelievers; . . .*
>
> *And now it came to pass that while he* (Alma) *was going about to destroy the church of God, for he did go about secretly with the sons of Mosiah seeking to destroy the church, and to lead astray the people of the Lord, contrary to the commandments of God, or even the king—* (Mosiah 27:8,10).

We know that as these men were pursuing their goal to destroy the church that an angel of the Lord appeared to them, calling them to repentance.

> *. . . for great was their astonishment; for with their own eyes they had beheld an angel of the Lord; and his voice was as thunder, which shook the earth; and they knew that there was nothing*

save the power of God that could shake the earth and cause it to tremble as though it would part asunder (Mosiah 27:18).

The Lord had their attention, and they responded by seeking repentance and undoing or trying to repair all that they had done to destroy the Church by corrupting lives. The visitation of the angel was an invitation to repent, but it did not make the requirements of repentance any easier for them.

> . . . (Alma and Mosiah's sons) *traveling round about through all the land, publishing to all the people the things which they had heard and seen, and **preaching the word of God in much tribulation, being greatly persecuted by those who were unbelievers, being smitten by many of them*** (Mosiah 27:32, emphasis added).
>
> *And they* (the four sons of Mosiah) *traveled throughout all the land of Zarahemla, and among all the people who were under the reign of king Mosiah, **zealously striving to repair all the injuries which they had done to the church, confessing all their sins, and publishing all the things which they had seen, and explaining the prophecies and the scriptures to all who desired to hear them*** (Mosiah 27:35, emphasis added).

These four sons grew up and were educated in the home of a righteous king, likely having been taught in all the ways of loving sons, loyal to Christ and Father, and faithfulness in aligning their lives with God's will. Yet, they chose the path advertised and designed by Satan as unbelievers, not as wondering bystanders, but forceful advocates desiring to destroy the Church. We don't know if their efforts were a consequence of pride, anger, or another festering destructive attitude. We do know that whatever it was, their actions bear testimony to the satanic deception they initially embraced.

Thankfully, when faced with light and truth presented in a way they could not ignore, they chose to become meek. They faced with determination all the challenges that would be theirs, moving from darkness into the light, unprotected from the view of the world. There was no shortcut, no easy way, having to pay the price that meekness and repentance required of them, even being sons of a king. In full view of their world, friend and foe alike, and through the required repentance process God was able to use their softened hearts and genuine covenants to bless the lives of others, many of whom had followed them earlier in unrighteousness. The price they paid to turn to the light was very challenging, but with their determined spirit, God was able to provide blessings to many.

> *And thus they were instruments in the hands of God in bringing many to the knowledge of the truth, yea, to the knowledge of their Redeemer.*
> *And how blessed are they! For they did publish peace; they did publish good tidings of good; and they did declare unto the people that the Lord reigneth* (Mosiah 27:36-37).

Their example confirms that when we choose to be meek, to turn from the spirit of the world, God is then able to use us to provide blessings not only for us, but for others, to complete the mortal mission we were each given in Father's home. We must all learn and embrace the truth. Truth and the Savior's light are essential to receive Eternal Life.

An invitation to come unto Christ and Father will come to each of Father's children in one way or another. It could begin with Father's children bearing witness, through the scriptures, through life experiences, and for some perhaps it may come from heavenly messengers. No matter how the invitation comes, it will come in a way that the recipient is capable of receiving it and will be confirmed by the Spirit. It isn't surprising then that the sons of Mosiah were filled with the desire to personally make this invitation to as many of God's children as they could, even though the discomforting rumor of what earlier had taken place must have made its way through the land.

> *Now they were desirous that salvation should be declared to every creature, for they could not bear that any human soul*

*should perish; yea, even the very thoughts that any soul should
endure endless torment did cause them to quake and tremble.*

*And thus did the Spirit of the Lord work upon them, for they
were the very vilest of sinners. And the Lord saw fit in his infinite
mercy to spare them; nevertheless they suffered much anguish of
soul because of their iniquities, suffering much and fearing that
they should be cast off forever* (Mosiah 28:3-4).

In continuing a review of the lives of Mosiah's sons following their
conversion, we see them desiring to go among the Lamanites, the sworn
enemy of the Nephites, which they did for many years, experiencing the
conversion of thousands. Their faithfulness and successful efforts bear a
solemn witness to the power and ability God blessed them with to fulfill
the stewardships and missions God called them to, but conversion had
to come first with payment of the price that repentance required of
them.

Becoming meek was a significant part of the "foundation" each
needed to assist Father and Jesus Christ in Their work. So, it is with
each of God's children, meekness is required, no matter what service
He calls them to, be it thought large or small, all will have redeeming,
transforming power.

I have witnessed this gift of spiritual power and understanding in
my own family with the child one might not expect to witness these
manifestations in. My only daughter, the oldest child, was born with
congenital heart disease. At the time of her birth, it appeared that her
body was starved for oxygen for a short time and consequently she had
reduced intellectual abilities. Her heart had not developed fully and as
a result the pulmonary artery and main aorta had to be sown together,
and a hole created in the area joined to take the place of the right side
of her heart.

One of the effects of this condition was that she was very small in
stature, the size of an eight-year-old when she was 19. She could only
read on a first-grade level, matching her other cognitive abilities. As
with all of God's children, even with disabilities, she had a number of

gifts. There were two that people would soon notice after getting to know her, verbal ability and a meek demeanor. In fact, as I pondered on Mosiah 3:19, I realized that she was the embodiment of that scripture in our family.

One day at home, when she was about nine years old, the doorbell rang and she answered the bell, opening the door. My wife was in another part of the house and heard the doorbell, the door opening, and the door closing, all quite quickly. My wife rushed to and opened the door to find a ward priesthood leader standing there looking a little confused. The reason for his visit was handled and following the closing of the door, mother and daughter had a short training session on etiquette. When asked why she closed the door on the visitor, my daughter responded that he was a bad man and that had triggered her action. As you might expect, we were perplexed about our daughter's response, until a few weeks had passed. This priesthood leader left his pregnant wife for another woman.

Those who are meek become worthy of other blessings such as spiritual power and discernment.

> *And the remission of sins bringeth meekness, and lowliness of heart; and **because of meekness and lowliness of heart cometh the visitation of the Holy Ghost,** which Comforter filleth with hope and perfect love, which love endureth by diligence unto prayer, until the end shall come, when all the saints shall dwell with God* (Moroni 8:26, emphasis added).

When life's mission is complete and the time for judgement comes, what will be the reward for the meek?

> *. . . for none is acceptable before God, save the meek and lowly in heart* (Moroni 7:44, emphasis added).
>
> *Blessed are the meek: for **they shall inherit the earth*** (Matthew 5:5, emphasis added).

CHAPTER 12

⊰∘⟲⟳∘⊱

BEING HUMBLE

*. . . becometh as a child, submissive, meek, **humble** . . .*
(Mosiah 3:19, emphasis added)

Currently in our culture, being humble doesn't often seem to be a desirable trait, even as meekness is not. Erroneously, humility is often associated with being timid, poor, quiet, fearful, of little value, or without desirability. Assumptions may also be made that humility isn't found within someone who is strong, bold, successful, or unafraid as these characteristics are the opposite of humility. How far from the truth these misunderstandings are. However, humility is incompatible with pride.

What escapes understanding is that the humble spirit in a person opens the gateway and provides the foundation for other valuable character traits and qualities to develop, establishing perspective that is unattainable in other ways. When a person is truly humble, he or she is unafraid to review personal feelings, goals, and attitudes for desirability, appropriateness, and whether they are compatible with a relationship with the Savior. It is found in people who listen and accept counsel, receive and embrace responsibility, are willing to learn and to make changes.

Can a person be both humble and bold, humble and courageous? Are these terms mutually exclusive like humble and arrogant? No, they are not. In fact, in reading the histories of presidents of the United States of America, two often discussed names stand out as examples of being humble and courageous, George Washington and Abraham Lincoln. Both went about fulfilling their difficult stewardships with boldness, while seeking divine instruction and help. They were teachable and unafraid to make changes, components of humility.

We have other illustrations in the scriptures of the application and outcomes of these qualities. Alma and the sons of Mosiah are examples we have already reviewed. Consider the Apostle Paul, who was a very active participant in the persecution of Christians. He took part in the martyrdom of Stephen, who had faithfully proclaimed truth to the Sanhedrin, the supreme council of the Jews. Moses, who was raised by Pharaoh's daughter and became the prophet that led the Israelites out of Egypt is another example.

Both Paul and Moses had to repent in order to fill the stewardships they were given. With this as a background, we can readily see that being humble is a key component in repentance, as they turned their lives around and embraced the mission each was given. They were called to commit themselves for years in the work of spiritual rescue and conversion. They met the challenges that tried their faith: testimony and resolve, humility guiding the exercise of faith, hope, trust, and patience. They were determined to keep their word and promises made to the Lord.

Having these marvelous examples, we can see that humility is an essential quality to fulfilling stewardships. What is the meaning of humble as used by King Benjamin? To gain the same understanding that he brought to this scripture, we must recognize that he used *becometh as a child* as the underlying basis for the instruction. So, how is it that being humble is a character trait of children?

Everything is new to a child. Hopefully, learning, growing, becoming proficient, changing, and trusting are all accepted parts of life as a child, all from the foundation of humility. Children discover the necessity to learn, practice, obey, and make changes as required. If these attributes are not learned as a child, the need does not disappear, as we are still required to learn as children do, to align our lives with truth, with Jesus Christ.

The process of humility's refining of the soul will require repentance for the changes that are needed in our lives. Repentance is a core component leading to a person's progression on the covenant path and is a necessary companion to all the attributes that align us with Father's will. As perfection has eluded all of us, repenting, accepting counsel, and striving to be obedient are efforts needed every day. These acts, fueled by righteous desires, refine our souls for genuine humility to develop and influence the completion of our life's mission. This should not be a surprise as the simple answer about humility's place in life is that it is a requirement of faithfulness and progression.

Try to imagine yourself having the same conversation with Christ that Peter had. Would His questions and responses to your answers be humbling in their effect upon you? Would you fear that your weaknesses, sins, and other matters that have found a place in your soul, would be exposed? The Savior already knows you, your strengths and weaknesses, your gifts and sins, even as He knew Peter's. Yet, the Savior stood ready to assist Peter in becoming what their combined efforts could make of him. So also, this blessing is available to all of us if we are willing to align our lives with Christ and His commandments.

Hopefully, we have done or will yet do as Peter did, expressing our love for Jesus Christ and embracing His instruction with faith and determination for obedient completion. This is the requirement made of us today, those of us who have been admitted into the kingdom of God here on earth, having received the saving ordinances of baptism, confirmation, endowment, and sealing to our families. For those who have not yet received and embraced these ordinances, the invitation continues as the requirements are still in place in order to be admitted into the kingdom and worthy of all the blessings available to Father's children, even Eternal Life.

Who will feed the Savior's lambs and sheep during our mortal mission? The Savior could have been speaking directly to us as He did Peter and has through His ordained apostles and prophets. We are to feed them (John 21:15-17). We have the responsibility and acting upon it we will receive the gifts, abilities, and orchestration of events and relationships as needed.

The blessing of being humbled and embracing humility with all our souls prepares us to make eternal, life-improvement changes necessary to be worthy to be in the kingdom and in God's presence. Whether Peter needed this application of humility for other types of changes, we do not know. We do know that he recognized what Christ was teaching and aligned himself with the Master Teacher for the completion of Peter's earthly mission. This is also what we must do.

> *And Jesus called a little child unto him, and set him in the midst of them,*
>
> *And said, Verily I say unto you, Except ye be converted, and* **become as little children,** *ye shall not enter into the kingdom of heaven.*
>
> **Whosoever therefore shall humble himself as this little child, the same is greatest in the kingdom of heaven.**
>
> *And whoso shall receive one such little child in my name receiveth me* (Matthew 18:2-5, emphasis added).

There is a tenderness in the vision this scripture inspires that softens the heart, perhaps filling the soul with a desire to be like that little child. Having that yearning, there seems to be a natural progression to receive *one such little child* in His name, for the blessing that follows from receiving Him, all the while striving to *become as little children.*

It is clear that becoming humble as a little child is a requirement to return Home. Humility describes a condition of the soul that changes who we are and how we connect with Father, Jesus Christ, and all of God's family. Without it, we cannot build strong and empowering relationships with them. Conversion will come and deepen as light fills the soul, usually not in a single experience, but progressing throughout life. Humility is a key. It is that important.

CHAPTER 13

⋯○⋐᠅⋑○⋯

BEING PATIENT

*. . . becometh as a child, submissive, meek, humble, **patient**
. . .* (Mosiah 3:19, emphasis added)

The Savior is the embodiment and essence of the many meanings of patience. From waiting until 30 years of age to be able to publicly exercise His Godly gifts and complete the mission given Him by Father, committing the last ounce of physical, emotional, and spiritual strength He possessed in the garden and on the cross to meet the demands of eternal law, He is the perfect example. He completed the Atonement, making it efficacious for all of Father's children. His exercise of patience cannot be duplicated and is a testimony to all of us of the need for patience in our lives.

Comprehension of His example may be beyond our understanding, but that doesn't mean we shouldn't follow Him to the best of our abilities with continued striving. We can do much, but often we may give ourselves an undeserved "pass," saying that being patient isn't one of our gifts. Whether it is a gift or not, we are required to put forth the effort to obtain it and use it.

On November 1, 1831, a special conference of elders of the Church was held for discussion of several items of business. One of the principal subjects was the publication of the revelations Joseph Smith had received from the Lord. Section 67 of The Doctrine and Covenants was received at that time.

> *For no man has seen God at any time in the flesh, except quickened by the Spirit of God.*
>
> *Neither can any natural man abide the presence of God, neither after the carnal mind.*
>
> *Ye are not able to abide the presence of God now, neither the ministering of angels; wherefore,* **continue in patience until ye are perfected** (D&C 67:11-13, emphasis added).

If any person wondered about the efficacy and need for patience daily, this scripture makes it very clear that it is needed now and until we are perfected or become complete. As we know, perfection is not possible for us in mortality, so patience and all its applications are required for our time here. No more excuses.

Scriptural instruction has been given to awaken us to Father's expectation and that this quality needs to become part of who we are. It is integral to the exercise of faith, becoming meek, humble, and filled with love. There is value in the processes of working to gain these personal attributes and other qualities that require time and repetition, for they then refine the soul. To understand its importance in blessing our families and gaining Eternal Life, consider the spirit and message of these scriptures.

> *Nevertheless the Lord seeth fit to chasten his people; yea, he* **trieth their patience** *and their faith* (Mosiah 23:21, emphasis added).
>
> *And now I would that ye should be humble, and be submissive and gentle; easy to be entreated;* **full of patience and long-suffering;** *being temperate in all things; being diligent in keeping the commandments of God at all times; asking for whatsoever things ye stand in need, both spiritual and temporal;*

always returning thanks unto God for whatsoever things ye do receive (Alma 7:23, emphasis added).

*And seek the face of the Lord always, that **in patience ye may possess your souls,** and ye shall have eternal life* (D&C 101:38, emphasis added).

When a person embraces the scriptures and seeks the necessary refining of his soul, there are three areas of obvious focus for exercising patience and long-suffering that are required in life, both temporal and spiritual: being patient in adversity, patient in striving, and patient in accomplishment. The scriptural instruction we have was written in brevity, but powerful in its clarity. However, there is more, much more to be understood and embraced individually. The depth and breadth of meaning comes not only from the words themselves, but from the Spirit as we prayerfully ponder and listen with faith. Father knows all our needs and will make the application personal for you and your family.

Patient in Adversity

One thing that each of us can count on in our lives is adversity. It might come from decisions we make or by the decisions of others. It might come individually or globally, but it will come.

We hope to be prepared with a defense, with sufficient strength, tools, and mind frame to deal with it. We know that Father and Christ use trials to strengthen and test us. Faith, hope, prayer, determination, and stamina are often put to active application.

Hopefully, we are sufficiently humble and meek to learn from the trials of others, as well as our own.

The Nephite people under the rule of King Limhi had hoped they were safe from the Lamanites' anger. They were not and King Limhi made a covenant with the Lamanite king to give up one half of all they possessed and one half of their increase in flocks and food to save their homes and lives. The scripture reveals that the Lamanite captors would go as far as they could get away with in persecution, without taking the Nephite's lives, in order to keep the oath their king made. They would *smite them on their cheeks, and exercise authority over them; and began to put heavy burdens upon their backs, and drive them as they would a dumb ass* (Mosiah 21:3).

There was no way that King Limhi's people could deliver themselves from this slavery. The afflictions they were suffering became so intense that the people wanted to go to war to get rid of their oppressors. Finally, King Limhi agreed to let them try. They went to war and were defeated. Motivated by the cries of the widows, they went to battle again and were defeated. They went a third time with the same outcome.

Finally, the people submitted once again to this bondage and a continuation of the same discouraging treatment. This time, however, they humbly turned to God.

> *And they did humble themselves even in the depths of humility; and they did cry mightily to God; yea, even all the day long did they cry unto their God that he would deliver them out of their afflictions.*
>
> *And now the Lord was slow to hear their cry because of their iniquities; nevertheless the Lord did hear their cries, and began to soften the hearts of the Lamanites that they began to ease their burdens; yet the Lord did not see fit to deliver them out of bondage.*
>
> *And it came to pass that they began to prosper by degrees in the land, and began to raise grain more abundantly, and flocks, and herds, that they did not suffer with hunger* (Mosiah 21:14-16).

The impatience of these people regarding their sufferings drove them to battle three times and many were killed, leaving numerous widows and fatherless children who had to be taken care of by others. The Lord was prepared to help them, but only when their **patience in affliction** led them to turn to Him with full purpose of heart and the humble exercise of faith, trusting the Lord to help them.

Another example of being patient in adversity occurred with the sons of Mosiah. After having experienced conversion and changing their lives as needed for repentance, they were filled with desire to bless lives instead of encouraging spiritual rebellion and sin. They determined to take the gospel to the Lamanites, their sworn, traditional enemy.

> *And the Lord said unto them also: Go forth among the Lamanites, thy brethren, and establish my word;* **yet ye shall be patient in long-suffering and afflictions,** *that ye may show forth good examples unto them in me, and I will make an instrument of thee in my hands unto the salvation of many souls* (Alma 17:11, emphasis added).

The work of this ministry required much in the way of trials for those who went among the Lamanites as they served 14 years with these people. They endured being stripped of their clothes and cast into prison, having little food and water, being driven from one location to another, verbal and physical abuse, yet they endured all this with **patience** and faith, leading to the conversion of thousands.

These sons of Mosiah were on a mission, determined to do all they were capable of to invite, instruct, and support the miracle of conversion of the Lamanites. Patience was required and exercised, no matter the afflictions they had to endure. What about us in our everyday lives? Are we justified in being impatient as we labor in instilling the blessings and promise of dedication and conversion in the lives of those we serve? Are these two examples just special cases and we shouldn't have to worry about being patient in affliction?

> *And not only so, but we glory in tribulations also: knowing that* **tribulation worketh patience** *(Romans 5:3, emphasis added).*

This statement from the writings of the Apostle Paul to the Roman saints summarizes one of the blessings of tribulations in our lives, even as we attempt to do right and bless the lives of our families and others. Challenges, trials, tribulations, whatever the descriptions are provide the power, force, and effective opportunity for developing the Godly quality of patience, among others.

We don't have to review the lives of very many people striving to be obedient to learn that it is a requirement of faithfulness to endure and grow from the many life challenges imposed on any one individual. Consider the faithful women and men in history. A review of their lives often reveals many difficult challenges that played a significant role in strengthening, refining, and enlarging their lives. Perhaps this depth of growth and progression is not possible without trials.

Consider people you know that have been anxiously engaged in being faithful "children." Have they been able to escape these difficult refining influences? How about Joseph Smith and those who were determined to follow his leadership in establishing the Lord's kingdom on the earth once again. Was their path made easy, because of what they were engaged in doing? Absolutely not!

Patience was an essential requirement. They were determined to meet, unwearyingly if needed, what became rigorous tests which facilitated the further development of individual strength and ability. Trials are tools Father uses to prove and refine His children. It is impossible to escape them if you desire to be a good person, a faithful child.

Perhaps an inventory of the challenges you and your family have met may be similar to my family. Here is a short list of mountains that had and still must be climbed and rivers that had to be forded: depression, anxiety, heart surgeries, untimely death, miscarriage, insomnia, bankruptcy, divorce, death of a child, job loss, dementia, loneliness, loss of hope, physical deformity, and other disabilities. What I have not listed are the blessings, miracles, and joys that far overshadow any of these difficulties. Under Father's and Christ's care, tribulations can and will be turned to blessings.

Patient in Striving

> ***Waiting patiently on the Lord***, *for your prayers have entered into the ears of the Lord of Sabaoth, and are recorded with this seal and testament—the Lord hath sworn and decreed that they shall be granted* (D&C 98:2, emphasis added).
>
> *Nevertheless, Jacob, my firstborn in the wilderness, thou knowest the greatness of God; and he shall **consecrate thine afflictions for thy gain*** (2 Nephi 2:2 emphasis added).
>
> *But if we hope for that we see not, then do we **with patience wait for it*** (Romans 8:25, emphasis added).
>
> *Now we exhort you, brethren, warn them that are unruly, comfort the feebleminded, support the weak, **be patient toward all men*** (1 Thessalonians 5:14, emphasis added).

My daughter, whom I described earlier and had congenital heart disease with several accompanying disabilities, passed away when she was twenty. She was promised in her Patriarchal Blessing that she will have children. We knew at the time the blessing was given that this promise wouldn't be fulfilled in mortality, because of her health situation. She was faithful all her life, lifting many who had even a small relationship with her. At the viewing prior to her funeral service, the line of visitors who wanted to talk with us was so long, we didn't know how we would be able to greet them all.

We heard stories of love, affection, blessings, and impact from this little soul who was filled with the Light of Christ and so totally divorced from the spirit of the world. We were in a state of awe and thanksgiving. How did we merit having such a choice soul as one of our children? My daughter spent all her life striving to be faithful, to bless others, and to fulfill her life's mission, patient in all things, knowing that she was different from others. That blessing by a faithful patriarch is in place and will be fulfilled according to the promise given and her continuing exercise of patience and faith.

Patient in Accomplishment

> **For ye have need of patience**, *that, after ye have done the will of God, ye might receive the promise* (Hebrews 10:36, emphasis added).

The blessings that await God's children as promised for their faithfulness must be voluminous and beyond our comprehension. There are milestones in every life, points in time, achievement recognized, success noted, and witness made signifying progression along the desired path our Father has for each of us, with specific points of reference on the covenant path.

Accomplishment does not necessarily signal that we have "arrived," that this is our final destination, only that we are in the right place and making our way to that trusted place God is directing us to. There may be many points on our journey when we are blessed to see our accomplishments and progression, but many more may remain in place, because we have not yet arrived at the designated point on the journey. Blessings that have been promised will be given according to our faithfulness, perhaps not when we think they should, but God keeps His word and will bless us at the optimum times for receipt.

If at any time or place on the journey, it has been a struggle and taxed our abilities to the point that we feel exhausted, even empty, staying where we are may be a great temptation. We may want to go no further, feeling we may need a little healing rest. However, staying may not be the plan for us. Being patient regarding God's desires and trusting Him to get us where He wants us is vital to our sanctification and returning Home.

There is scripture designed to assist us in achieving our righteous goals, providing a heavenly culture in which to see ourselves, where we've been, and where we are going.

> *There is a law, irrevocably degreed in heaven before the foundations of this world, upon which all blessings are predicated—*

86

And when we obtain any blessing from God, it is by obedience to that law upon which it is predicated (D&C 130:20-21).

And, if you keep my commandments and endure to the end you shall have eternal life, which gift is the greatest of all the gifts of God (D&C 14:7).

I, the Lord, am bound when ye do what I say; but when ye do not what I say, ye have no promise (D&C 82:10).

And if thou art faithful unto the end thou shalt have a crown of immortality, and eternal life in the mansions which I have prepared in the house of my Father (D&C 81:6).

The Lord spoke with clarity. The requirement for patience and continuance is significant in these scriptures and the one which follows. The instruction applies to all of Father's daughters and sons.

For whoso is faithful unto the obtaining these two priesthoods of which I have spoken, and the magnifying their calling, are sanctified by the Spirit unto the renewing of their bodies.

They become the sons of Moses and of Aaron and the seed of Abraham, and the church and kingdom, and the elect of God.

And also all they who receive this priesthood receive me, saith the Lord;

For he that receiveth my servants receiveth me;

And he that receiveth me receiveth my Father;

And he that receiveth my Father receiveth my Father's kingdom; therefore all that my Father hath shall be given unto him (D&C 84:33-38).

All of Father's children, both daughters and sons, who thankfully receive priesthood authority and order their lives with it unto the filling and magnifying their various callings in life will receive all that Father has, including Eternal Life. How do we even begin to comprehend such a blessing? Yet, that is the promise. What price must be paid by us, what challenges met with faith?

Verily I say unto you my friends, fear not, let your hearts be comforted; yea, rejoice evermore, and in everything give thanks;

*Waiting **patiently on the Lord**, for your prayers have entered into the ears of the Lord of Sabaoth and are recorded with this seal and testament – the Lord hath sworn and degreed that they shall be granted.*

Therefore, he giveth this promise unto you, with an immutable covenant that they shall be fulfilled; and all things wherewith you have been afflicted shall work together for your good, and to my name's glory, saith the Lord (D&C 98:1-3, emphasis added).

No matter what challenges life presents us, they all become personal, for we are required to meet them with patience and faith. If we do this, our righteous prayers will be heard by Father and granted according to need for our well-being, all according to God's will and timing. This promise is secure.

CHAPTER 14

BEING FULL OF LOVE

. . . becometh as a child, submissive, meek, humble, patient,
full of love *. . .* (Mosiah 3:19, emphasis added)

Love is our soul's genuine desire and need. Whether we recognize it or not our souls yearn to love and to be loved. Love is like food for our spirits, not just a pleasing snack, but a necessary full course meal to be consumed, embraced, appreciated every day, and returned. Love is a life sustaining and strengthening nutrient influence that invites and facilitates the receipt of other life empowering nourishment for our souls. It is endowed with temporal and spiritual qualities that make it one of the unique powers in our lives that when we give it way, we receive much more in return.

Pure love is sacred, having been given and received in our premortal Home, coming with us to mortality as an endowment from Heavenly Parents, being modeled and bestowed by Christ. It is a spiritual connection that blesses the giver and the receiver. Even though it is a shared, common, everyday emotion, found everywhere, it does not lose its value, if given and received in its purity. The commonality is a blessing. It should be received with thanksgiving and given liberally and widely, even beyond our comfort zones.

Its influence and eternal qualities inspire the receipt and unification with other eternal powers such as faith and hope, those that bridge distance, time, and opposition to provide blessing in the lives of others and us. The exercises of love become freewill gifts directed by Jesus Christ to the enhancement of people we do not know, as well as those who are active participants in our lives. This happens when we exercise love and righteous desire for them, for everyone, giving away what we freely receive.

Our beginnings in Father's home came about through love. We were raised and taught in love. Temporal life was created because of Father's and Christ's love for us, desiring that we progress and mature to be worthy of what They have and to become like Them. Love is a part of who we are. Love is a driving force for those who desire Eternal Life.

Love is so integral to godhood that Satan in his rage, rebellion, and expulsion from Father's home has promoted deceit and distractions continuously to demean its value and use. He cunningly attempts to lead us away with counterfeits that will not fill this need that is so fundamental to who we are. When we allow ourselves to be deceived and led astray, we turn from God's love and efforts to bring us Home. Without love we cannot progress sufficiently to be worthy of His kingdom, to be in His presence.

Children come to earth with love as a natural attribute, influencing all their interactions with others and their perception of life. Satan attempts to suffocate this blessing early in our lives. He has been so successful in promoting interferences and imitations that they seem a natural part of life, even desirable to some. People are constantly encouraged to look away from love by the adversary, unfortunately forgetting and in danger of losing this gift they come to mortality with. This doesn't change its necessity.

Sadly, the need in our souls may be filled with something that is a counterfeit, incapable of providing satisfaction and fulfillment. Regrettably, all the "noise" about us as proffered by the world likely bears a false witness that what we are feeling is love, when it is not, and is what everyone feels. That is a deceit of enormous depravity. To realize this should be enough for us to begin the effort to turn away and focus on the truth.

What happens to the love we were sent to earth with under this barrage of deceit; especially if we do nothing about it? Consider how we are tempted to embrace ideas or things to extremes to the exclusion of investments in love for something that is promoted as more delightful or fashionable, but is ultimately corruptive and destructive to the soul. Ponder the anger and selfishness promoted as desirable, including sexual temptations paraded in front of us 24/7.

The world promotes thoughts and attitudes that face inward rather than outward, as something we owe ourselves, because we deserve it. Satan has deceived many who are producers, advertisers, and customers. Temptation gets attention for all the wrong reasons.

The challenge of embracing and nurturing love can be difficult in this atmosphere. Love may have been hidden by the deluge of falsehoods being promoted all around us. Love may very well appear to have died or have been moved out of its place, from a lack of support when we allow the spirit of the world to influence our thoughts and desires.

However, love is a component of who we are and it can be summoned once again, strengthened by righteous influences, and blossom into the spiritual power it was designed to be. We need it to guide and enhance our lives and relationships. Knowing that mortal life is full of these valueless and fraud-inspired encouragements, we must, in the Lord's way, protest what we cannot control by our exercise of faith and energy to build fortresses of righteousness around our families and ourselves.

How many people do you know that love their careers, hobbies, leisure or other activities to the exclusion of time, commitment, and personal investment in relationships with family members and/or God? Let's not forget that counterfeits are designed by the adversary for our destruction. They can be very inviting to the "natural" disposed person. Our weaknesses and desires are known by those pushing Satan's agenda. That is why the temptations feel so personal and even desirable. There is powerful exploitation at the heart of them.

To turn from darkness unto light may require "baby steps," but turn we must. We must be ever watchful of the path ahead of us. That is one of the reasons why being on the covenant path is so valuable. Baptism is the ordinance that places us on the path. We take upon us the name of Jesus Christ, make covenants to remember Him and keep His commandments. We are reminded every week in taking the sacrament of these promises we have made and where we are going. Turning from the world to the Savior will give us clarity regarding what is in front and all around us, far different from the picture the adversary paints.

Our own disobedience, which we must own up to (because perfection has eluded all of us), may have insulated us somewhat from recognizing and receiving the truth. Begin with practical applications, praying for those things you can perform that will change you, if you have decided your life needs improvement.

When followed, they will prepare you to accept love from God and for God, as prompted by the Spirit. This is a necessity. If we do so, this will permit love to flower and blossom in order to influence all our thoughts and actions. Consider this scripture.

> But I say unto you, Love your enemies, bless them that curse you, do good to them that hate you, and pray for them which despitefully use you, and persecute you;
>> That ye may be the children of your Father which is in heaven: . . . (Matthew 5:44-45).

If our souls are filled with love, if we truly love others, we are likely to do as the Savior instructed. We can love a person without loving their decisions and actions, loving her or him because the person is a child of God. When we do this, loving as the Savior loves will come more naturally. We call this love charity, *the pure love of Christ* (Moroni 7:47).

Since the power of the spirit of the world has likely attempted to condition our feelings and attitudes to lead us away from this true love, we may need to find our way back by genuinely performing exercises and actions of faith that will begin the purifying process of yielding our hearts unto God.

Step by step, these exercises of faith and trust will bring us closer to the Savior, bringing about the sanctification of our souls until we are one with Father and Jesus Christ. Loving, blessing, praying, and doing good to those who are hard to do this for will transform who we are, and then we will come to know what true love is for it represents who we have become.

> *He that loveth not knoweth not God; for God is love* (1 John 4:8).
>
> *If a man say, I love God, and hateth his brother, he is a liar; for he that loveth not his brother whom he hath seen, how can he love God whom he hath not seen?*
>
> *And this commandment have we from him, That he who loveth God love his brother also* (1 John 4:20- 21).
>
> *Thou shalt love thy wife with all thy heart, and shalt cleave unto her and none else* (D&C 42:22).
>
> *Jesus said unto him, Thou shalt love the Lord thy God with all thy heart, and with all thy soul, and with all thy mind.*
>
> *This is the first and great commandment.*
>
> *And the second is like unto it, Thou shalt love thy neighbour as thyself* (Matthew 22:37-39).
>
> *By this shall all men know that ye are my disciples, if ye have love one to another* (John 13:35).
>
> *For God so loved the world, that he gave his only begotten Son, that whosoever believeth in him should not perish, but have everlasting life* (John 3:16).

The scriptures are full of the testimony of God's love for all His children. His love is not withdrawn regarding those who struggle or are disobedient. In fact, that is all of us, perhaps to a greater or lesser degree, but that is who we are. Father provides every opportunity and assistance to help each child find her or his way Home, if that is their desire. This pattern testifies of His love, and this is the pattern parents and family members should have for each other.

We all have the potential to be lighted beacons upon a hill, fueled by love that remains bright to light the path for a return for those who wander.

True love is based upon true principles, even as faith is. True love begins with the Father of us all and the Savior, for their love is given to all of Father's children. The prophet Moroni taught this principle.

> *And I am filled with charity, which is everlasting love . . .* (Moroni 8:17).

When we receive Father's and Jesus Christ's love with all our hearts, that "true love" is the example, the pattern, the seed that will grow into love within us, inspiring and empowering each of us to love as They love, to have charity – the pure **love for** Christ and the pure **love of** Christ.

> *. . . wherefore, the Lord God hath given a commandment that all men should have charity, which charity is love . . .* (2 Nephi 26:30).

These scriptures are a perfect guide to the thoughts and actions we should embrace as we strive to learn to love as the Savior loves, and for our progression on the path of life.

With this love, the giver is anxious to lift burdens, not only of family and immediate friends, but of all others he or she has contact with, even those they do not know. This person employs empathy for all of Father's children, caring about individuals, recognizing and feeling their pain and their challenge.

The scriptures' descriptive term is compassion. It is the core value of love. The compassionate person is willing to sacrifice to bless someone's life. Prayers are offered, sometimes continuously, for the blessings needed. The ongoing application of faith, hope, and service are all outcomes of the exercise of the desire to love as Jesus Christ loves and this love is no respecter of persons. All of Father's children are embraced within it.

Having no boundaries, love lasts forever. Consider this instruction from Jacob as he taught the people of Nephi.

> *O all ye that are pure in heart, lift up your heads and receive the pleasing word of God, and* **feast upon his love;** *for ye may, if your minds are firm,* **forever** (Jacob 3:2, emphasis added).

It should not be a surprise that the qualification required to *feast upon God's love* and to do so *forever* is striving to be *pure in heart*. This grand key provides that we will always have Christ's name and life in remembrance, continually, to be pure in heart, to be a true disciple, to receive and give love as Christ does. His image and name must always be in our hearts and on our minds, giving shape, color, and understanding to life and all that it is composed of.

When this is the state of our relationship, we will be filled with love for Christ, for all of Father's children, and have the strength and abilities needed to fulfill every stewardship and mission we are given to complete in mortality. Love invites obedience, devotion, and sacrifice.

CHAPTER 15

∞∘C～◯∘∞

WILLING TO SUBMIT

*. . . becometh as a child, submissive, meek, humble, patient, full of love, **willing to submit to all things which the Lord seeth fit to inflict upon him** . ..* (Mosiah 3:19, emphasis added)

This is the last quality, the last characteristic King Benjamin listed as a distinguishing feature of children. What is it designed to accomplish?

For the natural man is an enemy to God, and has been from the fall of Adam, and will be, forever and ever, unless he yields to the enticings of the Holy Spirit, and putteth off the natural man and becometh a saint through the atonement of Christ the Lord . . . (Mosiah 3:19).

The entire conversion process is designed to transform us from being the "natural man or woman" to becoming a saint. This is done by instructing us to become as children and yield to the enticing or invitations of the Holy Ghost. This can only be done through the Atonement of Jesus Christ.

96

As you look about you in the world and more specifically in your small part of it, it is not difficult to find people who are facing very difficult challenges, perhaps for much of their lives. Possibly you are one of these people. There is a temptation that may settle within the mind of some of God's children, who are striving to live faithful lives, to feel that life should get less challenging the closer one gets to aligning themselves with Christ's will. They may feel that peace, as it is imagined to be protection from mortal challenges, should be their reward.

The observation of Father's children throughout history does not confirm this rationale. In fact, those who we might assume are close to the Lord, often are dealing with mortal issues that might seem like punishment rather than blessing. It is important for each of us to keep in mind the Lord's work, *to bring to pass the immortality and eternal life of man* (Moses 1:39).

What preparation is needed for any one of His children to be worthy of the blessings of being in His presence and receiving the gift of Eternal Life? What changes must be made here in mortality? Father and Jesus Christ know what is needed for each of us and we must exercise sufficient faith that whatever we suffer here in the way of challenge will become a blessing for us as we strive to humbly and patiently meet each individual trial.

We left our pre-mortal home incomplete or imperfect as we might describe ourselves. We had weaknesses and needed much in the way of nurturing, education, and experience. Father's plan for us included a temporal life without memory of our prior existence to inspire a desire for understanding and growth reaching to the depths of our souls, hungry for truth and light. We have been given the Light of Christ and the Gift of the Holy Ghost to encourage the application of revealed understanding of our experiences relative to who we are and His desires for us.

We are required to search for truth and apply it in a worldly culture or atmosphere that often demeans spiritual truth and enlightenment. Carnal, tempting substitutes are pressed upon us daily by the adversary, lacking any nourishment for our souls. If we choose the substitutes and do not turn away from them, they will ultimately become destructive to us. To meet God's expectation of us, we have to be committed, ever willing to strive for what we truly need. This effort, fueled by desire and love, facilitated by truth and light, has the power to transform us, no matter what we have had to endure or suffer in aligning ourselves as "one" with Father and Jesus Christ. Even if we have chosen badly, we can correct our course and effort through repentance.

King Benjamin described this requirement as being –

> . . . *willing to submit to all things which the Lord seeth fit to inflict upon him* (us), *even as a child doth submit to his father* (Mosiah 3:19).

Submitting is the action that evidences our willingness to follow the Savior in all that life presents us, even the most difficult of challenges down to those that seem small or insignificant; not the submittal to a greater physical force, but one that often communicates in whispers that have the clarity and power to touch our hearts and minds together, the power to refine.

> *And it came to pass when they heard this voice, and beheld that it was not a voice of thunder, neither was it a voice of a great tumultuous noise, but behold, it was a still voice of perfect mildness, as if it had been a whisper, and it did pierce even to the very soul* (Helaman 5:30).

Satan extends temptations designed to turn us from submitting and some may be very powerful in their invitation to turn from the Light. However, God has made this promise:

> *There hath no temptation taken you but such as is common to man: but God is faithful, who will not suffer you to be tempted above that ye are able; but will with the temptation also make*

a way to escape, that ye may be able to bear it (1 Corinthians 10:13).

There are no qualifications given in this instruction to provide a way out of certain uncomfortable and hard-to-bear life events. It is interesting that King Benjamin instructed in being submissive and then in the same scriptural verse became more specific about readily submitting to all that Christ is willing to permit or orchestrate that will impact us, *submissive . . . willing to submit to all things which the Lord seeth fit to inflict upon him.* "Willing" suggests submitting in faith, not defiance or anger, in all the experiences life requires of us.

The sources that generate our experiences are varied – physical and mental make-up, gifts and abilities, decisions we make, decisions others make, and Heavenly orchestration of life involvement. Experiences may range from joyous and pleasurable to undesirable and painful. All provide temporal learning experience and will be used by the Lord for our benefit and blessing if we trust Him to make them productive and valuable. Otherwise we will miss recognizing and embracing them. Earth life is temporary, but with value to prepare us for life that does not end.

> *Verily I say unto you my friends, fear not, let your hearts be comforted; yea, rejoice evermore, and* **in everything give thanks;**
> *Waiting patiently on the Lord,*
> *. . . all things wherewith you have been afflicted shall work together for your good and to my name's glory, saith the Lord* (D&C 98:1-3, emphasis added).

Notice the instruction for patience. Intrinsic to life is the value of experience led preparation for the future and for the glory of God. We may judge experiences to be positive or negative, but all will be used for our blessing and progression if we are patient, humble, and exercise faith as instructed in the following scripture.

And if men come unto me I will show unto them their weakness. I give unto men weakness that they may be humble; and my grace is sufficient for all men that humble themselves before me; for if they humble themselves before me, and have faith in me, then will I make weak things become strong unto them (Ether 12:27).

Hopefully, you have experienced the fulfillment of these two scriptures personally. The goal, the expectation is that hope and trust have developed sufficiently within you to propel you forward, trusting that your faith will not fail and that you will continue to turn under the Lord's grace that which is negative into positive and weakness to strength.

Without question, prayer is essential for this progression to take place, including keeping a prayer in our hearts that binds us continually with the heavens from one moment to another. It is important to recognize that to meet the challenges of mortal life, proving faithful, there are two influences that must be in our hearts and minds continually, prayer and Jesus Christ.

If you were to catalog your weaknesses and afflictions, most likely there will be many. This will be the same for all of us children. Mortality has no favorites and does not provide perfection, but the opportunity to meet all different kinds of challenges, whether by our own hands or others. Each will have the same ultimate purpose, the preparation, growth, strengthening, and progression needed for all of life's components, as we strive to walk faithfully on the covenant path. Terrible tragedies and challenges may fall upon anyone, but if we trust God to get us where we need to be, even calamities and misfortunes will be turned to blessings in the lives of those trusting the Lord to help them.

Sometimes we may be tempted to say, "God doesn't care about me. I no longer have His love. He wouldn't allow this to happen to me if He loved me." The scriptures bear a different witness, revealing that He is a loving God, engaged in tough love at times to encourage the changes needed, not by force, but by our own experiences submitted to with awakening, evaluation, decision and commitment, supported by meaningful help and love. God respects our agency.

> *For God so loved the world, that he gave his only begotten Son, that whosoever believeth in him should not perish, but have everlasting life* (John 3:16).
> *A new commandment I give unto you, That ye love one another; as I have loved you, that ye also love one another* (John 13:34).
> *If ye keep my commandments, ye shall abide in my love; even as I have kept my Father's commandments, and abide in his love* (John 15:10).
> *He that hath my commandments, and keepeth them, he it is that loveth me . . .* (John 14:21).

The Savior's witnesses in these scriptures bear testimony of the place and power of love in each of Father's children and the responsibility we have to each embrace that love. The blessings we will receive for doing so, include not only receiving Father's and Christ's love, but that Christ will manifest himself to us. We will never be asked to "submit ourselves" without the blessing of God's love.

> *Therefore, sanctify yourselves that your minds become single to God, and the days will come that you shall see him, for he will unveil his face unto you, and it shall be in his own time and in his own way, and according to his own will* (D&C 88:68).

Ask yourself these questions. Are you willing to submit yourself to all things which are afflicted upon you with patience and faith? Are you willing to trust God that he will make the good and bad, all your experiences, into blessings for you? There is no picking and choosing. Willingness to submit is essential to our progression and requires the conviction to say to God, "I am thankful for all things."

Now, a concise look at King Benjamin's instruction. As you have read and pondered on the qualities that are essential for us, being children of a God and needing to exercise the simple faith and trust of children, there is a progressive relationship in these qualities. As we look at them, we realize that in submitting, becoming meek, humble, patient, and full of love, all are necessary components to prepare us to *submit to all things which the Lord seeth fit to inflict upon* us. This is necessary for His children to be worthy and prepared to return Home and receive the gift of Eternal Life.

CHAPTER 16

———◦∘C∾ᴗ∾◦∘◦———

THE LOVE OF PARENTS

It is difficult to conceive what life would be like without parents and the love they provide as new lives are brought into the world. The organizing of a family with children may feel like just a random outcome of nature, but how wrong that supposition is. There is design, organization, and even the working of miracles to provide parents, love, and succor for each of their children as they come into mortality. That is the design, but because mortality is not perfect, the organizing and progression of families is not perfect either. Mistakes are made, choices are not error free, and sins are committed.

Even though there are failures, successes are abundant, and provision is made through divine assistance for every new life to be blessed, for mistakes and poor choices can become nutrients for the seeds of blessing and success to sprout.

The design is for each child to be conceived in love that is everlasting, succored and guided to maturity, so that all that has been experienced and learned can be replicated over and over again, providing the blessings needed for each child. In this way children come to know who they are, who Father and Jesus Christ are, and they provide these blessings for those that follow.

Sons and daughters marry according to the design. It is intended that they will respectfully and lovingly establish family culture and prepare their children to follow their example in love and righteousness. Each parent has the opportunity to progress in the stewardship responsibilities that are theirs, some unique to their gender.

Parents are taught to become "one" in the establishment and operation of the family and home. They partner with God in the bearing of children, strengthening of families, and the ongoing nurture of children, being bound in love for time and eternity as family members receive the saving ordinances, such as baptism.

Parents have the opportunity to align themselves with Father and Jesus Christ in gaining the wisdom and understanding required for each child's development and progression to the fulfillment of their individual responsibilities and lives, both parents and children. Awakening, striving, sacrificing, and serving in humility with all the energy of soul become the everyday experiences of loving parents.

Is this designed pattern so different from the example Father set for us pre-mortally, for us to follow in mortality? Father's children have been and are continuing to be sent on this temporal journey which began with Adam and Eve. When that journey is completed, will they be returning Home? This question has been pondered ever since Adam and Eve became the first mortal parents for Father's children. Where did we come from? Is earth life all there is? Is there a home for us to return to when the mortal journey is over?

The scriptures have wonderful, God-given instruction for us to embrace and ponder, all available through the love of God.

Consider this revelation given to the prophet Moses by the Lord about the creation of the world and its population of Father's children.

For I, the Lord God, created all things, of which I have spoken, spiritually, before they were naturally upon the face of the earth . . . And I, the Lord God, had created all the children of men; and not yet a man to till the ground; for in heaven created I them; and there was not yet flesh upon the earth (Moses 3:5).

The creation of earth and its population have also been revealed to other prophets, providing multiple witnesses that we are the spirit children of Father, having lived with Him in His heavenly home.

> *Behold, the Lord hath created the earth that it should be inhabited; and he hath created his children that they should possess it* (1 Nephi 17:36).
>
> *For we saw him, even on the right hand of God; and we heard the voice bearing record that he is the Only Begotten of the Father—*
>
> *That by him, and through him, and of him, the worlds are and were created, and the inhabitants thereof are begotten sons and daughters unto God* (D&C 76:23-24).

The scriptures reveal that a loving God, our Father, provided instruction and preparation for His children before sending them to earth to gain physical bodies and essential experience for their progression. Certainly, all were tutored in Father's home. Many were diligent in following the Savior and other leaders (those considered noble and great), some were not. Importantly, each diligent child is blessed having the potential and opportunity to become heirs with Jesus Christ of all that the Father has. If we are to be heirs and glorified, then we have a responsibility to learn and strive to be valiant, following Christ's example and instruction from those consecrated to be apostles, prophets, and teachers.

> *Now the Lord had shown unto me, Abraham, the intelligences that were organized before the world was; and among all these there were many of the noble and great ones* (Abraham 3:22).
>
> *Before I formed thee in the belly I knew thee: and before thou camest forth out of the womb I sanctified thee, and I ordained thee a prophet unto the nations* (Jeremiah 1:5).
>
> *I* (President Joseph F. Smith) *observed that they* (Joseph Smith and other modern-day prophets) *were also among the*

noble and great ones who were chosen in the beginning to be rulers in the Church of God.

Even before they were born, they, with many others, received their first lessons in the world of spirits and were prepared to come forth in the due time of the Lord to labor in his vineyard for the salvation of the souls of men (D&C 138:55-56).

Does not all of this preparation and organization bear witness of a loving, caring, and merciful parent, our Father?

For God so loved the world, that he gave his only begotten Son, that whosoever believeth in him should not perish, but have everlasting life (John 3:16).

But behold, the Lord hath redeemed my soul from hell; I have beheld his glory, and I am encircled about eternally in the arms of his love (2 Nephi 1:15).

Lehi made this last statement when he was instructing his family, as recorded in the Book of Mormon. He recognized what the Apostle John also understood regarding the blessing of Eternal Life for those who will follow Jesus Christ.

Is not the love that Father has for us and His example of exercising that love a pattern that we should follow as families here in mortality? We are Father's children, and He had us taught and prepared pre-mortally to come to earth and experience life with a physical body. This brought new challenges and wonderful experiences. Some of these experiences can be especially trying, because we have no memory of that preparation, but they are still a part of each of us, hopefully contributing to our recognition of love, truth, and light, encouraging our loyalty and obedience.

In order for the experiences leading to the discovery of truth and expansion of our personal growth, we have been required to start this new life without the memory of a prior life. We have each been given the means to receive instruction here, prove it for its value through the Light of Christ and the Gift of the Holy Ghost, while striving to come to know what we knew pre-mortally. We have parents whose responsibility is to provide the example and support we need to receive, embrace, apply this truth, experience conversion, blossom in becoming who Father wants us to be and ultimately fulfilling the mission given to each of us. Each mission has value.

Families were organized and designed to provide the nurturing, support, and education of each of the children that would be sent to parents. Doesn't this follow the example and pattern set in our heavenly home, where we had parents nurturing us for the life that lay ahead? We were taught truth there. The truth is being taught here and the means to prove it are available to us, to differentiate it from all that is waste.

This is essential as we are surrounded by opposition designed to thwart Father's plan and efforts. Just as we were prepared for a new life pre-mortally, we are to be taught and prepared here for a new life that will yet come. Just as we had the responsibility of agency in Father's home, we have been given agency here and the blessings that can be given are subject to the decisions we make.

Now as you look around you, how often do you see this ideal model of parenting in place, operating according to its heavenly design? Perhaps, what you encounter is the application in various forms and stages of development and progression. Some situations may touch your heart with sadness for obvious challenges family members are dealing with, others filling your heart with joy for what is being accomplished and many more at different places all along this continuum of education, experience, and conversion, hopefully that all children are making their way to the Tree of Life. The Savior's love is not just reserved for two parent families, but for all, for all need His love and support.

Many families will embrace attitudes and lifestyles that appear to have been designed by the source of all opposition to Father's plan. Even as there is much to do and experience as individuals in mortality, there is much to learn and apply for the preparation of our families to receive the blessings, including joy, which awaits them for choosing wisely and exercising true love.

Perfection will elude our grasp as individuals and families, but our Father and the Savior are the source and embodiment of love, example and instruction. It is Their desire to bless us with all the blessings They can give as we progress in gaining the ability to receive, appreciate, and use Their marvelous gifts. Let's not lose sight of the fact that all our families are part of one family, Father's family.

The love and care provided by Father and Christ are intended to be mirrored here by parents and others, love being the central power providing protection, guidance and energy needed for care and progression. It binds us with unity to our ancestors, our posterity, and with Christ and Father. Our integrity and loyalty to God are essential as parents, as family members, expressing and truly giving love, wrapping our love around all that we think, say, and do, so that it resembles Christ's love.

CHAPTER 17

━━━━━━━━━ ◇○C〜○◇ ━━━━━━━━━

FROM CHILD TO SAVIOR

> *But inasmuch as they keep not my commandments, and hearken not to observe all my words, the kingdoms of the world shall prevail against them.*
>
> *For they were set to be a light unto the world, and **to be the saviors of men;***
>
> *And inasmuch as **they are not the saviors of men,** they are as salt that has lost its savor and is thenceforth good for nothing but to be cast out and trodden under foot of men* (D&C 103:8-10).

Some background on the above scripture. Section 103 of the *Doctrine and Covenants* was given through Joseph Smith following the arrival of Parley P. Pratt and Lyman Wight in Kirtland, OH. They came to counsel with the Prophet regarding the relief the Missouri saints needed after losing their lands in Jackson County. The instruction in these verses makes it very clear that the saints were to be not only a "light" for others, but to be "saviors" as well.

According to the Merriam-Webster Online Dictionary the first definition of a savior is someone who "saves from danger or destruction." Using this definition, any person on the earth could potentially qualify as a savior, a rescuer in a mortal sense. The second definition adds an essential qualification, "one who brings salvation." To bring salvation, the person must be endowed with truth, light, and authority as required.

Jesus Christ is known as the Savior, He whose mission to lift and save mankind from the challenges of sin, from outcomes of corruption being furiously sought by the adversary. Christ is the supreme example of the qualities and responsibilities of being a savior.

> *Behold, I am Jesus Christ the Son of God . . . I am the light and the life of the world. I am Alpha and Omega, the beginning and the end* (3 Nephi 9:15, 18).

He **lives**. He **reigns**. He **saves**. He **loves**. He **forgives**. He **unburdens**. He **strengthens**. He **obeys**. He **sacrifices**. He **atones**. He **lifts**. He **invites**. He **visits**. He **answers**. He **refreshes**. He **creates**. He **protects**. He **awakens**. He **weeps**. He **testifies**. He **calls**. He **sanctifies**. He **befriends**. He **waits**. He **lights**. He **inspires**. He **leads**. He **chastens**. He **restores**. He **reveals**. He **commands**. He **serves**. He **joys**. He **descended**. He **arose**. He **answers**. He **reveals**. He **governs**. He **judges**. He **heals**. He **teaches**. He **opens** (the windows of Heaven).

> *. . . for there is none other name under heaven given among men, whereby we must be saved* (Acts 4:11).

Jesus Christ makes salvation available to all of Father's children. He is the source of all truth and light, whose very character is essential to the process of salvation. This is how immortality was brought about and the act of shepherding God's children is ongoing, leading them to make the decisions to be worthy to return Home and enjoy Eternal Life. To assist God in this work is to become a savior and is the calling of all those who have willingly received Jesus Christ and gospel truth. From becoming "as a child" to progressing to be a savior appears to be the natural path for those who desire to assist the Lord in His work within their families and for others in Father's greater family.

Our prior examination of the scriptures provided the instruction that we are to become as children to have the right mental and spiritual attitudes for the development necessary to become saints and return Home to Father. As we embrace it, that progression will fill our souls with all that is needed to follow Jesus Christ's example and to become saviors ourselves.

> *And if it so be that you should labor all your days in crying repentance unto this people, and bring save it be one soul unto me, how great shall be your joy with him in the kingdom of my Father!*
>
> *And now, if your joy will be great with one soul that you have brought unto me into the kingdom of my Father, how great will be your joy if you should bring many souls unto me* (D&C 18:15-16).

This is the work of saviors!

The "child to savior path" examples are abundant. We can see them in the scriptures and all around us in the lives of faithful daughters and sons of God. Often these are people that we admire because of their humility, outpouring of love, relationship with the heavens, and willingness to bless everyone around them. Review the life of any of God's children who are striving to be faithful, true disciples of Christ and you will come to understand the core requirements of the path, including becoming as a child. Experiences and challenges may differ from one person to another, but the transformations they engineer will be those which are needed in each person's life.

Challenges are a key component in this Godly required tutorial. Ultimately, to become the child Father wants us to be, we will need to become wise enough to understand what challenges have done for us, even to embrace and give thanks for them. If we trust God to guide and help us through them, they will have been a tool that has refined our souls to receive innumerable blessings.

Thou shalt thank the Lord thy God in all things (D&C 59:7).

Verily I say unto you my friends, fear not, let your hearts be comforted; yea, rejoice evermore, and in everything give thanks;

Waiting patiently on the Lord, for your prayers have entered into the ears of the Lord of Sabaoth, and are recorded with this seal and testament—the Lord hath sworn and degreed that they shall be granted.

Therefore, he giveth this promise unto you, with an immutable covenant that they shall be fulfilled; and all things wherewith you have been afflicted shall work together for your good, and to my name's glory saith the Lord (D&C 98:1-3).

Search diligently, pray always, and be believing, and all things shall work together for your good, if ye walk uprightly and remember the covenant wherewith ye have covenanted one with another (D&C 90:24).

The Lord has made it very clear in scripture that He is aware of all things in our lives and will make them work for our good, if we have believing and thankful hearts. It is important for us to understand that we likely learn more from difficult challenges than from other kinds of mortal experiences.

Having to call on reservoirs of strength and understanding that we may not be aware of, learning new things, and being required to exercise and develop increased faith and trust when all may seem to be lost, are conditions and experiences that the Lord uses for our benefit and His glory, thus the commandment to *thank the Lord thy God in all things* (D&C 59:7).

In reading these scriptures and evaluating my own life experiences, I have come to realize that blessings always attend challenges. We will likely miss seeing them if we are so caught up in anger or frustration, feeling sorry for ourselves (Why me? I have been striving to be faithful!) or want to blame God for what has taken place, so that we are unwilling to look, recognize, and appreciate the blessings that are there for us to embrace.

To accept these "gifts" means we trust God to get us where we need to be, even if a great difficulty is in front of us and the required efforts are exhausting. Father's help will come in the way that provides the greatest blessing for us. Perhaps burdens will be made lighter or disappear with little attention from us. We may need to experience the full challenge of the problem, being required to exercise faith, trusting God that we will be able to work through the trial and that it will be a blessing. Whatever is best for us is what the Lord will do. Our responsibility is to trust Him to get us where we need to be. If we do so, we will be able to say with Nephi,

> *O Lord, I have trusted in thee, and I will trust in thee forever*
> (2 Nephi 4:34).

At the time of this writing, my wife and I are experiencing a challenge the like of which, well, it is one of the most difficult of our lives and it affects the two of us differently, but perhaps to the same important end. On April 17, 2022, Easter Sunday, my wife suffered a very severe stroke stemming from a deep brain hemorrhage.

The stroke occurred on the left side of the brain, resulting in the right side of her body being affected, including wiping out her ability to speak for several days, followed by aphasia, which is a communication disorder. She has lost fine motor control in her right hand (she is right-handed), a loss of feeling on the right side of her face, and is not able to walk normally, now having to drag her right foot.

I knew from the time of the stroke that the Lord was cognizant of the trial, but the unknown felt forbidding, and I couldn't help having a little fear that tugged on my heart and mind as I determined to trust the Lord that His will was being done. My hope was that blessings would be given and perhaps even miracles would be performed for her blessing. I didn't know what the outcomes would be, but because of other life trials and the witness of God's attention to our needs, I am exercising what strength I have to trust God to get both of us where we need to be. The challenge will require the exercise of faith, hope, humility, and love.

I was introduced to the role of being a full-time caregiver. I found that it requires much of whatever ability I have to give physically, emotionally, and spiritually. My prayer, beginning on that important day was for her blessing and mine, whatever God saw fit to bless us with. My heart at this time seemed encouraged to ponder on the Savior's Atonement and what was mandatory for Him to complete this greatest of all gifts for Father's children, the Atonement. Under eternal law, Jesus was required to sacrifice everything He could give physically, emotionally, and spiritually. He did it for the love of Father and us, and in obedience to Father's will.

As I have been required to labor, to sacrifice the abilities I have for the love of my sweetheart and in obedience to heavenly instruction, I have gained increased understanding and appreciation for the Savior's sacrifice in completing the Atonement. I can just begin, in a very small way, to relate to the cost of the Atonement and the love required and exercised by the Savior. This realization has been a personal blessing and has filled me with far greater love for Jesus Christ and the desire to draw near to Him.

Even facing the unknown, having no knowledge of how this will turn out, my soul is filled with thanksgiving for the challenge (which to some may be difficult to understand) and what I have learned in the process. I feel closer to the Savior and have felt His love transforming me. How could I be angry or have any complaint when Jesus Christ is in this experience? My wife does not. When asked how she is doing, she always answers "great." Great are God's blessings in our lives.

I know that I am not alone in facing this kind of experience and outcome. We can all progress on the path to becoming a savior by first becoming as a child and trusting God as we traverse along the path of mortal life. If we continue, we will be filled with the light Father desires for us and will exercise and use that light and the gifts we have been given to help lift the burdens of others, serving as saviors, following in spirit and deed He who is the Savior of us all, Jesus Christ.

I bear witness with Nephi that we must—

> *. . . press forward with a steadfastness in Christ, having a perfect brightness of hope, and a love of God and of all men. Wherefore, if ye shall press forward, feasting upon the word of Christ, and endure to the end, behold, thus saith the Father: Ye shall have eternal life.*
>
> *And now, behold, my beloved brethren, this is the way; and there is none other way nor name given under heaven whereby man can be saved in the kingdom of God. And now, behold, this is the doctrine of Christ, and the only and true doctrine of the Father, and of the Son, and of the Holy Ghost, which is one God, without end* (2 Nephi 31:20-21, three Gods, united as if one).

I trust that these two verses of scripture fill your soul with thanksgiving, awe, and love for Christ, having a desire to align your life with Him. It is important to notice from these verses that the *doctrine of Christ is man can be saved in the kingdom of God.* If you have never known or understood what Christ's doctrine is, this instruction makes it clear that Fathers' children can receive the gift of Eternal Life.

All of the Savior's efforts are designed to make that happen, upon pressing *forward with a steadfastness in Christ.* That should lift all our hearts and desires beyond earthly trials and rewards to *having a perfect brightness of hope,* while *feasting on the word of Christ.* This gift requires loving God and His children, and not giving up, enduring as the scripture instructs.

CHAPTER 18

ATTRIBUTES OF THE HEART

ttributes are qualities or characteristics of a person's heart. They determine how susceptible a person is to the receipt and embracing of truth, including trustworthiness to do the work of aligning their souls with Father's will and as true disciples of the Savior. It is through the heart that love is embraced and extended to others. Attributes are evidence of love for Jesus Christ that go far beyond lip-service and temporal manipulations. They open the heart, inviting and facilitating changes, growth, and the development of new attributes that become part of the person. In other words, new or expanded attributes can be acquired even though they did not earlier exist within the heart if the person *yields to the enticings of the Holy Spirit* (Mosiah 3:19).

King Benjamin's instruction in that verse was an encouragement for people to seek, develop, and totally embrace the attributes of being *submissive, meek, humble, patient, full of love, willing to submit to all things which the Lord seeth fit to inflict upon him.* If done so, the outcome would be putting *off the natural man* and becoming *a saint through the atonement of Christ the Lord* (Mosiah 3:19). These traits are essential to the establishment of the foundation needed to be faithful, loving children.

Their development and growth can be witnessed by observing a person's "fruits" or what the person says and does. In this regard, the Savior's instruction in the Sermon on the Mount, known as the Beatitudes, bears a powerful witness of the composition of a person's soul with this foundation in place if he or she exemplifies the "doing" of this divine education. The Beatitudes were taught in the old and new worlds as revealed by the Bible and Book of Mormon.

Think of the Beatitudes in this way—they are the outcomes when the righteous heart attributes direct what a person does in life.

> *Blessed are the poor in spirit (who come unto me* 3 Nephi 12:3): *for theirs is the kingdom of heaven.*
>
> *Blessed are they that mourn: for they shall be comforted.*
>
> *Blessed are the meek: for they shall inherit the earth.*
>
> *Blessed are they which do hunger and thirst after righteousness: for they shall be filled.*
>
> *Blessed are the merciful: for they shall obtain mercy.*
>
> *Blessed are the pure in heart: for they shall see God.*
>
> *Blessed are the peacemakers: for they shall be called the children of God.*
>
> *Blessed are they which are persecuted for righteousness' sake: for theirs is the kingdom of heaven.*
>
> *Blessed are ye, when men shall revile you, and persecute you, and shall say all manner of evil against you falsely, for my sake. Rejoice, and be exceeding glad: for great is your reward in heaven: for so persecuted they the prophets which were before you* (Matthew 5:3-12).

As can be seen, these outcomes require more than just "doing" in the temporal sense (without conversion), they require changing the heart (conversion) by embracing the needed spiritual characteristics. Our goal should be to align with God's will and work to become saints, true disciples, even saviors.

Jesus Christ's instruction in this sermon engaged many different topics. Let's examine a few and their relationship to heart attributes.

Salt of the Earth

>*Ye are the salt of the earth: but if the salt have lost his savour, wherewith shall it be salted: it is thenceforth good for nothing, but to be cast out, and to be trodden under foot of men* (Matthew 5:13).

In our day, this statement by the Savior may not have as much meaning as it did for those who heard Him speak. You may be aware that salt has been used as a preservative for millennia and is certainly used in our day as a flavor enhancer, having the ability to increase the depth of flavor of many different foods. However, salt continues to be used as a preservative around the world, even though there are other more modern methods for extending the life of foods.

>*All the heave offerings of the holy things, which the children of Israel offer unto the Lord, have I given thee, and thy sons and thy daughters with thee, by a statute for ever: it is a **covenant of salt for ever** before the Lord unto thee and to thy seed with thee* (Numbers 18:19, emphasis added).

A "heave" offering refers to the movement of the offering over the alter when sacrifices were made in Old Testament times. The properties of salt, using it as an analogy to make and keep covenants, provided a means of understanding for people throughout the ages that covenants with God are intended to be long lasting as evidenced by this scripture. Therefore, a "covenant of salt" implies that the covenant will have an everlasting nature, and the individual must change how he or she lives to keep from polluting the covenant. Salt loses its savor when it is mixed with other elements, thereby becoming contaminated. If the salt has lost its savor, there is no way that it can be returned to what it was. Salt must be kept pure, without contamination, to be effective.

For covenants to be effective, they must be kept as purely as we are able, without excuses and with the exercise of faith. We make covenants when we are baptized and all along the "covenant path" of obedience to God's instruction, receiving all the saving ordinances like the endowment and being sealed to family members. All are sanctifying ordinances with covenants being key components. We promise to be obedient, and God promises that we will receive all that is necessary to be prepared and worthy to return and be with Him.

The use of salt by the Savior in this instruction on the covenant to follow Him emphasized that if salt becomes polluted it isn't any better than the dirt people walk on. If God's children pollute the covenants they have made by choosing sin over obedience, of what value are they in the "work of the Lord," which should be their work? What kind of relationship will they have with Father and the Savior having polluted their covenants? Fortunately, repentance is available to all of God's children, being forgiven and cleansed, reversing the effects of pollution. Obviously, the salt analogy does not provide instruction regarding repentance, but it does emphasize the need for faithfulness, for purity to complete our mission in mortality.

> *Behold, he who has repented of his sins, the same is forgiven,*
> *and I, the Lord, remember them no more* (D&C 58:42).

Light of the World

The Lord in our day used this analogy in instruction regarding the members of the Church in Missouri, revealed to Joseph Smith in 1834.

> *For they were set to be a light unto the world, and to be the*
> *saviors of men;*
> *And inasmuch as they are not the saviors of men, they are as*
> *salt that has lost its savor, and is thenceforth good for nothing but*
> *to be cast out and trodden under foot of men* (D&C 103:9-10).

This is sobering instruction on the outcome of making covenants and the necessity of keeping them. What a contrast there is between being a *light unto the world, the saviors of men,* and being *cast out and trodden under foot of men.*

> *Ye are the light of the world. A city that is set on an hill cannot be hid.*
>
> *Neither do men light a candle, and put it under a bushel, but on a candlestick; and it giveth light unto all that are in the house.*
>
> *Let your light so shine before men, that they may see your good works, and glorify your Father which is in heaven* (Matthew 5:14-16).

How uplifting this teaching is! To be filled with light implies that we can be seen, recognized, and have value, because the light is within us, having received it from Jesus Christ, enlightenment that fills our souls. He is the source of all light and truth. We become able to radiate light by desiring, receiving, and embracing truth, including making and keeping covenants.

> *For the word of the Lord is truth, and whatsoever is truth is light, and whatsoever is light is Spirit, even the Spirit of Jesus Christ.*
>
> *And the Spirit giveth light to every man that cometh into the world; and the Spirit enlighteneth every man through the world, that hearkeneth to the voice of the Spirit* (D&C 84:45-46).
>
> *And the light which shineth, which giveth you light, is through him who enlighteneth your eyes, which is the same light that quickeneth your understandings;*
>
> *Which light proceedeth forth from the presence of God to fill the immensity of space—*
>
> *The light which is in all things, which giveth life to all things, which is the law by which all things are governed, even the power*

of God who sitteth upon his throne, who is in the bosom of eternity, who is in the midst of all things (D&C 88:11-13).

To be the "light of the world" testifies of those who have sought and joyously received the Light of Christ. It is incumbent upon all those receiving this light to let it shine before men, *that they may see your good works, and glorify your Father which is in heaven* (Matthew 5:16). To be sure, the Light of Christ can be recognized by others even though they may not understand what has caught their attention. This becomes an opportunity to assist them in understanding what they have witnessed and why they have received it.

Love

In Chapter 14, Full of Love, two verses from the Sermon on the Mount were reviewed concerning the Savior's instruction on love. Here, we will focus on all of Matthew 5:43-47.

> *Ye have heard that it hath been said, Thou shalt love thy neighbour, and hate thine enemy.*
>
> *But I say unto you, Love your enemies, bless them that curse you, do good to them that hate you, and pray for them which despitefully use you, and persecute you;*
>
> *That ye may be the children of your Father which is in heaven: for he maketh his sun to rise on the evil and on the good, and sendeth rain on the just and on the unjust.*
>
> *For if ye love them which love you, what reward have ye: do not even the publicans the same?*
>
> *And if ye salute your brethren only, what do ye more than others? do not even the publicans so?*

This instruction is so captivating and powerful in its comparisons. Following this lesson, which may have surprised many, the Lord compared the hearers to the hated collectors of taxes, the publicans, if they only return love to those who love them. The Savior expanded on the exercise of love to include even saying hello or acknowledging those who are not in this circle of loved associates. The instruction is poignantly expressed that we all should be doing much more to expand and include others in our circle of kindness and love.

Love your enemies. Bless them that curse you. Do good to them that hate you. Pray for them which despitefully use you, and persecute you. Why should they do this? Making this personal, why should we do this? Responding in this way may not have been common in the culture at the time of the Savior. Perhaps some in our day feel the same way. The answer for making these changes is resolved in our hearts and minds when we accept and determine to truly *be the children of your Father which is in heaven.* We are of one family. Love your brothers and sisters!

Many similar comparisons which attest to a description of the faithful enlighten our understanding that they deserve Father's blessings. However, Jesus pointed out that the sun rises on all of Father's children, the evil and the good, and rain falls on the just and the unjust. Father loves all His children and provides what is needed for them to make the most of their mortal journey. Christ instructs all to love as He loves. We don't have to approve of the decisions and actions of others, but we are required to love, to treat others with respect for us to be worthy to return Home and be in His presence, securing our place as His children.

This instruction from The Only Begotten Son of God invites prayerful pondering, consideration, and practice at length to love as He loves.

Prayer

And when thou prayest, thou shalt not be as the hypocrites are: for they love to pray standing in the synagogues and in the corners of the streets, that they may be seen of men. Verily I say unto you, They have their reward.

But thou, when thou prayest, enter into thy closet, and when thou hast shut thy door, pray to thy Father which is in secret; and thy Father which seeth in secret shall reward thee openly.

But when ye pray, use not vain repetitions, as the heathen do:
for they think that they shall be heard for their much speaking.
Be not ye therefore like unto them: for your Father knoweth
what things ye have need of, before ye ask him (Matthew 6:5-8).

This instruction bears a powerful testimony of how sacred and vital prayer is. It isn't to put on a show, to make someone appear to be great or to be manipulative in any way. Prayer is all about a genuine, sacred sharing of our hearts and minds, our needs, concerns, and joy with Father. It is all about creating a relationship in which we are anxious to receive His counsel, to be trustworthy to obey and become worthy of receiving that which Father desires to give us. In this we are aligning our lives with His will that we become worthy to return Home and be in His presence.

Genuine prayer requires humility, meekness, the exercise of faith, hope, and being eager to submit to Father's will.

If any of you lack wisdom, let him ask of God, that giveth to all men liberally, and upbraideth not; and it shall be given him.

But let him ask in faith, nothing wavering. For he that wavereth is like a wave of the sea driven with the wind and tossed (James 1:5-6).

Behold, verily, verily, I say unto you, ye must watch and pray always lest ye enter into temptation; for Satan desireth to have you, that he may sift you as wheat.

Therefore ye must always pray unto the Father in my name;

And whatsoever ye shall ask the Father in my name, which is right, believing that ye shall receive, behold it shall be given unto you (3 Nephi 18:18-20).

Draw near unto me and I will draw near unto you; seek me diligently and ye shall find me; ask, and ye shall receive; knock, and it shall be opened unto you.

Whatsoever ye ask the Father in my name it shall be given unto you, that is expedient for you;

And if ye ask anything that is not expedient for you, it shall
turn unto your condemnation (D&C 88:63-65).

These scriptures are just a small sample evidencing God's desire to counsel with us, to bless us, to give every needful thing that will be required to be worthy to return and be with Him. The giving of gifts is His desire. What does He require for our prayers to be heard and the gifts given? Genuine desire. Sincerity. Faith. Hope. To pray always, diligently. To ask for that which is right or expedient for us, trusting that He will bless us according to our need. To pray to Father in the name of Jesus Christ.

Read and ponder the prophet Alma's instruction to his son Helaman regarding prayer and how it should be used, including all that is a part of faithful prayer.

> *Yea, and cry unto God for all thy support; yea, let all thy*
> *doings be unto the Lord, and whithersoever thou goest let it be in*
> *the Lord; yea, let all thy thoughts be directed unto the Lord; yea,*
> *let the affections of thy heart be placed upon the Lord forever.*
>
> *Counsel with the Lord in all thy doings, and he will direct*
> *thee for good; yea, when thou liest down at night lie down unto*
> *the Lord, that he may watch over you in your sleep; and when*
> *thou risest in the morning let thy heart be full of thanks unto*
> *God; and if ye do these things, ye shall be lifted up at the last day*
> (Alma 37:36-37).

Alma's expressions are wonderful! They clearly identify how our relationship with Father and Jesus Christ should be. They identify clearly the elements of conversion and their application to be able to return Home.

Following the death of Alma and a period of conflict, war between the Nephites and Lamanites, a peace was restored. This became a time of great prosperity, yet the people did remember all the blessings the

Lord had given them, and they did not turn to pride as had happened in earlier times.

> And **they** (the people) **did pray unto the Lord their God continually,** insomuch that the Lord did bless them, according to his word, so that they did wax strong and prosper in the land (Alma 62:51, emphasis added).

Imagine the tender feelings that must have filled the hearts of the people as they prayed. They recognized the need and the blessings of having a strong, personal relationship with God, which was evidenced by their continual prayers.

The desire and practice of praying continually to our Father in the name of Jesus Christ are attributes and practices of true disciples. The practical application of righteous desire leading to prayer can be in place in our lives continually, but what about actually praying? The Savior answered this question when he appeared to the Nephites following His resurrection. His disciples, at His request, and all that were in attendance were praying with all the energy of soul as they had been instructed.

> And it came to pass that he commanded the multitude that they should cease to pray, and also his disciples. And he commanded them that they should not cease to pray in their hearts (3 Nephi 20:1).

That is the answer, and this instruction should be followed in our day, making it the pattern of our lives. The building of the relationship is up to us as Father and Christ will keep Their word. Follow this counsel day-to-day to be worthy to receive all the blessings Father has set aside for you, including the Gift of the Holy Ghost. Remember, His desire, His work is to give all His gifts to you, when you are ready to receive them. Without prayer and the continuous aligning of our lives through it with Father, we risk not being ready and worthy to receive.

Christ uttered this prayer in the presence of the multitude.

Father, I thank thee that thou hast given the Holy Ghost unto these whom I have chosen (the disciples)*; and it is because of their belief in me that I have chosen them out of the world.*

Father, I pray thee that thou wilt give the Holy Ghost unto all them that shall believe in their words.

And now Father, I pray unto thee for them, and also for all those who shall believe on their words, that they may believe in me, that I may be in them as thou, Father art in me, that we may be one (3 Nephi 19:20-21, 23).

Did you notice in verse 23 that Christ prayed for those who are converted that they will become one with Father and Him? Chapter 5, page 31 has more information regarding becoming "one."

The tender feelings that filled the hearts of the people as they prayed in Christ's presence are the same tender feelings that we can receive when we pray as they did, with humble, genuine hearts, anxious to draw near and align our lives with Christ. Tears are often a personal witness of the receipt of Father's tender mercies and the feelings that fill our souls.

Forgiveness

For if ye forgive men their trespasses, your heavenly Father will also forgive you:

But if ye forgive not men their trespasses, neither will you Father forgive your trespasses (Matthew 6:14-15).

In seeking forgiveness of our sins from Father, we know that repentance is mandatory. Repentance requires change, the very act with corresponding life change of turning from sin unto the Savior, unto truth and light. This evidences a significant change in our souls. By requiring us to forgive others to receive forgiveness, we will gain an understanding and appreciation of the role and desirability of godlike love and mercy. This should invite us to follow Jesus Christ's example and assist others in the healing of their souls as our soul also finds healing. Everything Father requires of us is designed for our progression and worthiness to receive Eternal Life.

> *My disciples, in days of old, sought occasion against one another and forgave not one another in their hearts; and for this evil they were afflicted and sorely chastened.*
>
> *Wherefore, I say unto you, that ye ought to forgive one another; for he that forgiveth not his brother his trespasses standeth condemned before the Lord; for there remaineth in him the greater sin.*
>
> *I, the Lord, will forgive whom I will forgive, but of you it is required to forgive all men* (D&C 64:8- 10).

Refusing or ignoring our responsibility to forgive is a sin. Notice that Jesus Christ in this instruction did not give any other qualifiers providing us an opportunity to refuse to forgive. As hard as this might be, we are required to forgive, and the number of times is without end. In some situations, we might have to work to adequately prepare to have our hearts aligned with God's will to genuinely give forgiveness. Perhaps ongoing prayer, pleading for the desire and ability to forgive will be required. Pride and selfishness will make it all the harder to accomplish. Don't give in to forgiving difficulty. Humility, meekness, and the application of charity facilitate being able to forgive, even forgetting what was said or done as charity heals and replaces anger.

Succor from Jesus Christ and the companionship of the Holy Ghost will be given as we invite these blessings into our lives by our sincere efforts to be obedient. The one being forgiven may choose not to receive the gift of foregiveness, but we will experience growth and change that brings us closer to the Savior, exchanging sin for blessing.

Treasures in Heaven

> *Lay not up for yourselves treasures upon earth, where moth and rust doth corrupt, and where thieves break through and steal:*

But lay up for yourselves treasures in heaven, where neither moth nor rust doth corrupt, and where thieves do not break through nor steal:

For where your treasure is, there will your heart be also (Matthew 6:19-21).

Mortality requires that we support our lives with work that will bring sustenance and security to us and others. Unfortunately, many of Father's children get so caught up in this effort that the spirit and proper place of it fades away and they don't recognize other blessings mortality was designed to supply—a holistic life, tempering the physical with the spiritual, for each child to have experiences that require decisions and efforts worthy of salvation. If our treasure is in the world, then that is where our heart and mind will lead us.

The fruits of these efforts beyond our needs of temporal support provide only that which is impermanent and of little potential value to bless our souls. Sadly, for many, treasures in heaven are not recognized at all or are misunderstood. The result for these people is that they have embraced a counterfeit and probably have spent much of their time, effort, and ability in something that is addictive, without value, and ultimately destructive unless they turn to the Light.

For what is a man profited, if he shall gain the whole world, and lose his own soul? or what shall a man give in exchange for his soul (Matthew 16:26)?

But wo unto the rich, who are rich as to the things of the world. For because they are rich they despise the poor, and they persecute the meek, and their hearts are upon their treasures; wherefore, their treasure is their god. And behold, their treasure shall perish with them also (2 Nephi 9:30).

Each of Father's children is given gifts designed to be used in mortality, gifts that will strengthen the soul and bless the lives of others if properly used. We get to choose how we use them. Some of these gifts, when applied for what the world can give, provide fruits for the investment of focus, time, ability, and effort. These fruits may include riches, honor, power, and others that are treasured temporally. These are often valued by the adversary for the temptations they provide to confuse and corrupt the souls of Father's children, if not balanced by spiritual comprehension. If these fruits become the person's treasure, taking the place of a relationship with God, the treasure becomes a false god supplanting a true Godly relationship.

> *Think of your brethren like unto yourselves, and be familiar with all and free with your substance, that they may be rich like unto you.*
>
> *But before ye seek for riches, seek ye for the kingdom of God.*
>
> *And after ye have obtained a hope in Christ ye shall obtain riches, if ye seek them; and ye will seek them for the intent to do good—to clothe the naked, and to feed the hungry, and to liberate the captive, and administer relief to the sick and the afflicted* (Jacob 2:17-19).

The Atonement with its incomparable blessings and the required sacrifice by the Savior is a singular event. The spirit of the sacrifice included a depth of love and devotion far beyond what mortals can comprehend. It embraces the desire to serve and bless individually each of Father's children with Eternal Life. The Christlike application in our lives comes about when without any thought of personal reward, we take the gifts and substance given us and share with others so *that they may be rich like unto us.*

There is no implication that we should become destitute in the blessing of others—only that we be wise and be willing to sacrifice regarding our real needs and share with others who have not, *for the intent to do good.* We have the responsibility to choose what that is and how much, but the spirit of blessing others suggests we follow the Savior's example to lift burdens. This is also known as "charity" or the "pure love of Jesus Christ."

Judge Not Unrighteously

Now these are the words which Jesus taught his disciples that they should say unto the people.

Judge not unrighteously, that ye be not judged; but judge righteous judgment (JST Matthew 7:1-2, Joseph Smith's translation).

For with what judgement ye judge, ye shall be judged: and with what measure ye mete, it shall be measured to you again.

And why beholdest thou the mote that is in thy brother's eye, but considerest not the beam that is in thine own eye (Matthew 7:2-3)?

The Savior has instructed all of us to "judge righteously." What attributes are part of a righteous judgment?

He hath shewed thee, O man, what is good; and what doth the Lord require of thee, but to do justly, and to love mercy, and to walk humbly with thy God (Micah 6:8)?

Through the prophet Micah, the Lord instructed that what He requires of us in order to follow Him is to deal justly, love mercy, and to be humble. To do so requires us to focus outside of ourselves and to treat others as we want to be treated. No matter what we witness another child of God doing or saying, we do not have the ability to know him or her as God knows the person. There may be burdens that are incredibly heavy to bear and we know nothing of them.

In no way can we compare ourselves to another person and use ourselves as the standard for judgment. Mercy and humility will not permit it. To be just, we must obey what is morally correct according to God's instruction. The outcome for unrighteous judgement is to have that same standard used for us. That only seems fair. Knowing this should give us pause when we find ourselves thinking or saying something that is negative about another.

Ask and It Shall Be Given You

Ask, and it shall be given you; seek, and ye shall find; knock, and it shall be opened unto you:

For every one that asketh receiveth; and he that seeketh findeth; and to him that knocketh it shall be opened (Matthew 7:7-8).

Gaining information and understanding sounds so simple. It is, if we are striving to be faithful as God is anxious to bless us with truth and light.

. . . for your Father knoweth what things ye have need of, before ye ask him (Matthew 6:8)

If any of you lack wisdom, let him ask of God, that giveth to all men liberally, and upbraideth not; and it shall be given him.

But let him ask in faith, nothing wavering, For he that wavereth is like a wave of the sea driven with the wind and tossed (Jame 1:5-6).

Yea, he that repenteth and exerciseth faith, and bringeth forth good works, and prayeth continually without ceasing—unto such it is given to know the mysteries of God (Alma 26:22).

It is essential that we each come to know that everything that is good, just and true, bears witness of Jesus Christ, that He lives; for He is the source of truth and goodness and knows what we need before we ask Him. Consistency in the exercise of faith is required for the receipt of that which we do not know, such as *the mysteries of God*. Without consistency, faith and works have no power to effect change in our beings and prove our worthiness to receive Father's blessings.

Moroni's instruction to come to know the truthfulness of the Book of Mormon (Moroni 10:4-5) provides a pattern for coming to know the truth of all things. There is only one way to know the truths and mysteries of God. They must be revealed by Him. As all are sacred, they will be revealed to those who are striving to be trustworthy.

The Lord requires our efforts to be genuine, to represent the desire of our hearts as we become responsible for what we receive. We must commit to live righteously with the truths He gives us. The bottom line is, if we embrace and hold sacred what we receive, we are blessed and prepared to receive more. If we choose not to be faithful regarding what is revealed, we will receive no blessing and must stand responsible for the judgment that will follow.

> *Therefore to him that knoweth to do good, and doeth it not, to him it is sin* (James 4:17).
>
> *For of him unto whom much is given much is required; and he who sins against the greater light shall receive the greater condemnation* (D&C 82:3).

If our desire is to come to know much, even the mysteries of God, then much will be required of us, not only in the receipt of sacred knowledge, but in how we use it and respect its use ongoing throughout our lives. Again, we must be trustworthy. We become responsible for the truths God gives us.

> *For behold, thus saith the Lord God: I will give unto the children of men line upon line, precept upon precept, here a little and there a little; and blessed are those who hearken unto my precepts, and lend an ear unto my counsel, for they shall learn wisdom;* **for unto him that receiveth I will give more; and from them that shall say, We have enough, from them shall be taken away even that which they have** (2 Nephi 28:30, emphasis added).

If we say we are not interested in receiving anything more, it is clear we will lose that which we have been given. This bears a solemn testimony of how important and sacred truth is as well as our personal progression and being trustworthy. If we thankfully receive truth, God will continue to give more as we progress sufficiently to receive it. Progress is Godly required change. This glorious method is required for us to eventually receive all the blessings Father has for his children, including Eternal Life. Asking is the first step to receiving. How vital that genuine step is.

When we begin our focused and determined walk down the "the straight and narrow way," these first attributes of the heart, *submissive, meek, humble, patient, full of love, willing to submit to all things which the Lord seeth fit to inflict upon him* (Mosiah 3:19), are essential to our personal foundation for acquiring and using all the attributes and actions given in The Sermon on The Mount.

These attributes assist the heart in becoming open to new awakenings, attitudes and activities. The heart invites the "new" and facilitates its embrace as the individual requests the Spirit to confirm the validity of the changes. With those in place, the attributes invite, fashion, facilitate, and assist with the life changes needed for us to become saints, true disciples of Jesus Christ (loving Him), and becoming saviors ourselves. This instruction should cause us all to ponder regarding our relationship with the Lord and what is expected of us as we receive that which is sacred and make it a part of our lives.

As you ponder upon the truths that are conveyed in these sacred instructions from Jesus Christ, there is one attribute that seems to be at the core of life, the influence that has the energy and power to cause us to look to the Savior and lift our feet, pressing forward on the covenant path. That attribute is love. It fills hearts, minds, and energizes all particles of our being to commit us to faithful following of the Plan of Happiness (Plan of Salvation), and the fulfilment of our individual mortal missions.

Loving Jesus Christ and Father with all our souls will align our lives with Their desires for us and propel us on to be worthy to be blessed with Eternal Life. That love will help us to bridle our passions, turn from the darkness and sins of the world, and to grab hold of the "iron rod" of truth to guide us to the Tree of Life.

Following Lehi's receipt of the vision of the Tree of Life and other things relative to life's journey, Nephi desired to know of the things which his father saw. During a vision, an angel appeared to guide Nephi regarding what he was seeing and experiencing.

> *And the angel said unto me: Behold the Lamb of God, yea, even the Son of the Eternal Father! Knowest thou the meaning of the tree which thy father saw?*
>
> *And I answered him, saying: Yea **it is the love of God**, which sheddeth itself abroad in the hearts of the children of men; wherefore, it is the most desirable above all things* (1 Nephi 11:21-22, emphasis added).

The blessings that God can give His children, who truly love Him, are described in this way by the Apostle Paul.

> *But as it is written, Eye hath not seen, nor ear heard, neither have entered into the heart of man, the things which God hath prepared for them that love him* (1 Corinthians 2:9).

CHAPTER 19

———⊷⦅◦◦⦆⊶———

THE SPIRIT SPEAKETH EXPRESSLY

For the natural man is an enemy to God, and has been from the fall of Adam, and will be, forever and ever, unless he yields to the enticings of the Holy Spirit . . . (Mosiah 3:19).

We have explored the sermon that completes the rest of this scriptural verse. Now, let's look at why King Benjamin says that *the natural man is an enemy to God.* It is important to remember that the "natural man and woman" are identified as the people who will not humble themselves, turning to God with repentance, anxiously seeking the Spirit, and who do not love Him with all their hearts. These people receive *not the things of the Spirit of God for they are foolishness unto them* (1 Corinthians 2:14).

The Apostle Paul appears to have seen our day with great clarity. He speaks boldly and specifically about the heart, attitudes, mind, and actions of the "natural man."

Now the Spirit speaketh expressly, that in the latter times some shall depart from the faith, giving heed to seducing spirits, and doctrines of devils;

Speaking lies in hypocrisy; having their conscience seared with a hot iron (1 Timothy 4:1-2).

In everyday language, we might say that in our day many people will depart from faith in Jesus Christ. They will embrace temptations and actions inspired by Satan, designed for turning from the Savior to the source of darkness and corruption. They may speak as if they are still faithful but have truly turned from the Source of Light and no longer love God.

Isaiah understood who these people are as the future was made known to him.

Wherefore the Lord said, Forasmuch as this people draw near me with their mouth, and with their lips do honour me, but have removed their heart far from me . . . (Isaiah 29:13).

We often speak of the Light of Christ as our conscience, having that quality of self-examination and evaluation, but as you read it appears to be much more than this temporal explanation. The Apostle John bore this witness, that Christ-

*. . . was the **true Light,** which lighteth every man that cometh into the world* (John 1:9, emphasis added).

Christ said of Himself-

*I am come a **light into the world,** that whosoever believeth on me should not abide in darkness* (John 12:46).

This gift is given to each of Father's children to assist them in awakening and discerning the truth of who they are, why they are here, and how they should live their lives in worthiness to return Home when that time comes.

For the word of the Lord is truth, and whatsoever is truth is light, and whatsoever is light is Spirit, even the Spirit of Jesus Christ.

And the Spirit giveth light to every man that cometh into the world; and the Spirit enlighteneth every man through the world, that hearkeneth to the voice of the Spirit.

And every one that hearkeneth to the voice of the Spirit cometh unto God, even the Father (D&C 84:45-47).

The Light of Christ will lead all to truth and receipt of the Gift of the Holy Ghost, the companionship of this member of the Godhead, who has the responsibility of revelation and sanctification, among others.

When a person no longer listens to and aligns his decisions and actions with his conscience or the Light of Christ, it is as if he had used a hot iron to sear (burn) and close off his conscious's ability to guide his thoughts and desires. This instruction is compared to using an instrument like a hot knife to stop the bleeding of a wound by pressing it upon the opening and searing the flesh together.

Consider the personal characteristics of these people, which are evident in our day.

For the love of money is the root of all evil: which while some coveted after, they have erred from the faith, and pierced themselves through with many sorrows (1 Timothy 6:10).

This know also, that in the last days perilous times shall come.

For men shall be lovers of their own selves, covetous, boasters, proud, blasphemers, disobedient to parents, unthankful, unholy,

Without natural affection, trucebreakers, false accusers, incontinent, fierce, despisers of those that are good,

Traitors, heady, highminded, lovers of pleasures more than lovers of God;

Having a form of godliness, but denying the power thereof: from such turn away . . .

Ever learning, and never able to come to the knowledge of the truth (2 Timothy 3:1-5, 7).

A myriad of evidences of these personal characteristics and actions is available every day through the news media and personal interaction. These souls are not just in someone else's city or place, but right here wherever we live. There is a personal side to this. At one time or another we may have been guilty of one or more of these characteristics.

Satan doesn't have to attempt to get us to access the whole lot of sinful activities to be successful in diverting us from the truth. He can choose one at a time, encouraging through fatigue, anger, hopelessness, loneliness, fear, desire for pleasure or relief, loss of self-worth or any other emotion that degrades our protection and wisdom to tempt us to just try one of them. This diverts our attention from the Light of Christ and the Holy Spirit.

The adversary just needs to make it look desirable at the time of our greatest pain, weakness, or lowest spiritual energy for the temptation to have its greatest impact. It is vital that we understand that our lives have value, recognizing temptations for what they are. We need to turn our backs on the enticement, focusing on Jesus Christ with full purpose of heart, repenting, forgiving ourselves and others, and trust the Savior to help us to come to our spiritual senses and embrace the Light.

The "natural person" refuses to do this. This list of natural person characteristics is damning. It is filled with so much darkness that it is hard to comprehend. The natural man's or woman's commitments and loyalties are such that Light is "foolishness" to them. If we begin to turn toward the Light and a spiritual awakening is accepted by us, then supporting experiences will come. Once embraced, we realize that repentance is real, and Jesus Christ's Atonement was performed for each of us. He is the Light and true happiness is only available when we follow Him.

The scriptures make it clear that Satan is an enemy to God and that he is exerting every effort to turn us from truth. His war with God is being waged to destroy God's plan, children, and to hurt his own Father.

. . . the devil, who is the master of sin, or who is the evil spirit which hath been spoken of by our fathers, he being an enemy to all righteousness (Mosiah 4:14).

Wherefore, men are free according to the flesh; and all things are given them which are expedient unto man. And they are free to choose liberty and eternal life, through the great Mediator of all men, or to choose captivity and death, according to the captivity and power of the devil; for he seeketh that all men might be miserable like unto himself (2 Nephi 2:27).

The "natural man" is an enemy to all righteousness and to Jesus Christ *the Great Mediator.* The Apostle James characterizes it another way, giving this word of caution.

. . . know ye not that the friendship of the world is enmity with God? Whosoever therefore will be a friend of the world is the enemy of God (James 4:4).

Enmity isn't a commonly used word. In this scripture it means being actively opposed or hostile to God. We see much around us that fits in with this characterization. James's comment about *being a friend of the world* is a reminder of this instruction from the Savior.

No man can serve two masters: for either he will hate the one, and love the other; or else he will hold to the one, and despise the other. Ye cannot serve God and mammon (Matthew 6:24).

Mammon is defined as the degrading stimulus of material wealth, the world's influence. A decision to serve God is the decision that must be made wherever we are on life's path. King Benjamin's rebuke of the "natural man and woman" is not without an escape, a way to correct the unfavorable life course - **unless he** (they) **yields to the enticings of the Holy Spirit** (Mosiah 3:19, emphasis added).

The Spirit will awaken and instruct, often with a whisper, a very quiet prompting, that won't be recognized if the person is not listening, so that God's desire is not forced on His child. This provides the opportunity to choose, first to listen, then to obey. Choosing is vital to progressing to Eternal Life.

> *And it came to pass when they heard this voice, and beheld that it was not a voice of thunder, neither was it a voice of a great tumultuous noise, but behold, it was a still voice of perfect mildness, as if it had been a **whisper**, and it did pierce even to the very soul* – (Helaman 5:30, emphasis added).
>
> *Yea, thus saith the still small voice, which **whispereth** through and pierceth all things* (D&C 85:6, emphasis added).

In contrast, it is important to remember that Satan is a master of imitation and will do all he can to mimic God's interactions with His children and confuse man into following him. He quietly whispers or trumpets, as needed, his own messages of temptation and untruth, striving to plant them securely on the stages of mortal minds.

> *And behold, others he flattereth away, and telleth them there is no hell; and he saith unto them: I am no devil, for there is none—and thus he **whispereth** in their ears, until he grasps them with his awful chains, from whence there is no deliverance* (2 Nephi 28:22, emphasis added).

It is vital to recognize where the whispers come from. God will not use a crooked course or deception to get you where you need to be. Nephi's brother, Jacob, explained it in this way.

> *Behold, the way for man is narrow, but it lieth in a straight course before him, and the keeper of the gate is the Holy One of Israel; and he employeth no servant there; and there is none other*

way save it be by the gate; for he cannot be deceived, for the Lord God is his name (2 Nephi 9:41).

A narrow, straight path means that we cannot wander very far and still be returning Home. The Holy Spirit is there to let us know if we are drifting off the path. That is the only way to return to where our journey began.

Alma explained the necessity in this way.

> *But behold, the Spirit hath said this much unto me, saying: Cry unto this people, saying—Repent ye, and prepare the way of the Lord, and walk in his paths, which are* **straight** (Alma 7:9, emphasis added).
>
> *For behold, it is as easy to give heed to the word of Christ, which will point to you a* **straight** *course to eternal bliss, as it was for our fathers to give heed to this compass* (Liahona), *which would point unto them a* **straight** *course to the promised land* (Alma 37:44, emphasis added).

We know what the promised land is for us, but we don't know all the stops and important decisions that we will have to make along the way. God does and the Holy Spirit is sent unto each life to assist, without taking over. We are in charge of our way forward or backward.

In my lifetime, I have experienced innumerable enticings of the Spirit in all areas of life. However, I didn't always recognize them at the time of the Spirit's whispers. On some occasions, thankfully I did. There was a time earlier in my life when I felt the intense desire to improve my knowledge and testimony of Joseph Smith as a prophet of God. I decided to go to a bookstore and see what books were available to help me. I still remember the shelf in front of me that contained many titles.

I began the search, scanning the titles and authors. I hadn't been at this labor very long when I came to the *Life of Joseph Smith the Prophet* by George Q Cannon. The Spirit spoke with a whisper, and I knew this was the volume I should read. Joy filled me immediately, knowing that my prayer was answered by the Spirit's instruction. This was another witness of Father's love for me. I read the volume and the promise I felt from the "enticing" of the Spirit was fulfilled. I was fed, strengthened, and my testimony deepened.

The Spirit does speak expressly or clearly. God does not deal in half-truths, guile, or any instruction that is designed to deceive. God speaks truth and enlightens the heart and mind with Light to recognize it. Follow the enticings of the Holy Spirit and you will be led to the Savior and the completion of the earthly mission you were given, especially the blessing and sanctification of your family members whether here or on the other side of the veil. These are outcomes invited and fueled by love.

~o⌒o~

CHRISTLIKE CHARACTER

The Lord made this proclamation to Joseph Smith regarding the saints who were sent to Jackson County, Missouri:

> *For they were set to be a light unto the world, and to be the saviors of men* (D&C 103:9).

The very thought of being a savior, of having sufficient truth and light to assist in blessing and inspiring others to reach out to Jesus Christ for salvation is a most sobering, yet inviting, even glorious opportunity.

It implies, even in our mortal state so filled with weakness, mistakes, misunderstandings, and imperfect struggles, that the blessings of salvation not only can be shared by us but must be. Jesus Christ is the supreme example of how the blessings of salvation are to be given by personal witness.

Can we develop a Christlike character to follow His example for us to be saviors? Yes! The childlike qualities of character we have discussed are certainly an essential foundation and must be further built upon. The scriptures bear a clear witness that this is part of the design of mortal progression.

Possibly you have heard someone described in this way, he or she has "good character." What is meant by this? The Merriam-Webster online dictionary contains a very detailed list of the many definitions of "character." Two that are very helpful in answering this question are:

- A person marked by notable or conspicuous traits
- Moral excellence and firmness

Both are representative of Jesus Christ. Consider these four components of Christ's character that may be "conspicuous" or foundational traits needed by anyone who is a disciple of Christ and desires to follow Him in blessing the lives of others.

Compassion

Jesus Christ's life and ministry, as revealed in the scriptures, meet both above definitions and provide a composite example of what our personal character should include to be one of His disciples. With that in mind, let's examine the book of Third Nephi within the Book of Mormon, where is recorded Jesus Christ's visit to the "new world."

The people had gathered around the temple in the land Bountiful following cataclysmic destruction that occurred after Christ's sacrifice and crucifixion. There, Christ appeared and taught those present, a blessing to the "many." After instructing in numerous redemptive principles, the Savior said,

> *I perceive that ye are weak, that ye cannot understand all my words which I am commanded of the Father to speak unto you at this time.*
>
> *Therefore, go ye unto your homes, and ponder upon the things which I have said, and ask of the Father, in my name, that ye may understand, and prepare your minds for the morrow, and I come unto you again.*
>
> *And it came to pass that when Jesus had thus spoken, he cast his eyes round about again on the multitude, and beheld they*

*were in tears, and did look steadfastly upon him as if they would
ask him to tarry a little longer with them.*

*And he said unto them: Behold my bowels are filled with
compassion towards you* (3 Nephi 17:2, 3, 5, 6).

He then instructed the people to bring any of their number who were
afflicted in any way to Him to be healed, a blessing to the "one." Having
compassion is a Christlike character trait. His compassion was focused
for both temporal and spiritual blessings. Many bear witness to His
love and the miracle of healing throughout the scriptures. Compassion
is a basic trait of those who follow the Savior's example and strive to be
disciples. The prophet Isaiah described Jesus Christ in this way.

*He is despised and rejected of men; a man of sorrows, and
acquainted with grief: . . . Surely he hath borne our griefs, and
carried our sorrows* (Isaiah 53: 3-4).

Matthew records that Jesus went about the countryside preaching
the gospel and healing.

*But when he saw the multitudes, he was moved with
compassion on them, because they fainted, and were scattered
abroad* (Matthew 9:36).

A leper came to the Savior, pleading that he be healed.

*And there came a leper to him, beseeching him, and kneeling
down to him, and saying unto him, If thou wilt, thou canst make
me clean.*

*And Jesus, moved with compassion, put forth his hand, and
touched him, and saith unto him, I will; be thou clean* (Mark
1:40-41).

Following the Savior's suffering in Gethsemane, He was confronted by several people who had come to arrest Him, including Judas who betrayed Him with a kiss. The disciples in that chaotic moment wanted to know what Christ wanted them to do.

> *And one of them smote the servant of the high priest, and cut off his right ear.*
> *And Jesus answered and said, Suffer ye thus far. And he touched his ear, and healed him* (Luke 22:50-51).

Upon the cross, suffering indescribable agony, the Savior's compassion was no less evident.

> *When Jesus therefore saw his mother, and the disciple standing by, whom he loved, he saith unto his mother, Woman, behold thy son!*
> *Then saith he to the disciple, Behold thy mother! And from that hour that disciple took her unto his own home* (John 19:26-27).

Both examples bear a powerful witness of Jesus Christ's compassion, His desire to lift burdens is so evident throughout the New Testament and all scripture. These last two examples provide an important introspective and revelatory aspect of Christ's character. In the first, a significant crisis is unfolding, and it is obvious that the natural response from the apostles may have been to fight. What does the Savior do? He says *suffer ye thus far,* meaning to accept what is taking place. Then He heals the right ear of the servant. The Savior's compassion never wavered, even in this very tense and difficult situation.

In the second example, the Savior has already gone through the incredibly painful and exhausting sacrifice in the Garden of Gethsemane. Now, He is on the cross, paying the required sacrifice of His life through the most horrific execution the Romans could devise. It is from this platform that He secures care for His mother from the Apostle John.

In both instances, Jesus Christ's focus was not inward, but outward—always seeking the welfare of others before considering His own. It is an intriguing question to ponder on how we might have responded. A savior must have an outward focus. The will of God must be more important than our own desires and comfort. This is a vital component of Christlike character for each of His disciples.

Prayerful

Jesus Christ clearly established how beneficial and essential prayer is throughout His mortal ministry and following His resurrection as He interacted with many of Father's children, instructing and ministering. He counselled with Father through prayer, requesting blessing for those He ministered to and established His obedience to Father's will.

> *Therefore, hold up your light that it may shine unto the world. Behold I am the light which ye shall hold up—that which ye have seen me do. Behold ye see that I have prayed unto the Father, and ye all have witnessed* (3 Nephi 18:24).

Some may wonder about the efficacy of prayer. We must suppose that there is a difference between genuine prayer, those that are offered in humility and fervent desire, and those that provide only lip service or are only a spur of the moment offering. Father hears our prayers and both Father and Son respond to our needs if we truly yield our hearts unto Them and do so through earnest desire and prayer.

> *. . . for your Father knoweth what things ye have need of, before ye ask him* (Matthew 6:8).
> *Behold, verily, verily, I say unto you, ye must watch and pray always lest ye enter into temptation; for Satan desireth to have you, that he may sift you as wheat.*
> *Therefore ye must always pray unto the Father in my name;*

And whatsoever ye shall ask the Father in my name, which is right, believing that ye shall receive, behold it shall be given unto you (3 Nephi 18:19-20).

Draw near unto me and I will draw near unto you; seek me diligently and ye shall find me; ask, and ye shall receive; knock, and it shall be opened unto you.

Whatsoever ye ask the Father in my name it shall be given unto you, that is expedient for you (D&C 88:63-64).

If any of you lack wisdom, let him ask of God, that giveth to all men liberally, and upbraideth not; and it shall be given him (James 1:5).

The effectual fervent prayer of a righteous man availeth much (James 5:16).

And all things, whatsoever ye shall ask in prayer, believing, ye shall receive (Matthew 21:22).

Pray always, and I will pour out my Spirit upon you, and great shall be your blessing (D&C 19:38).

. . . ye shall pray unto the Father in the name of Christ, that he will consecrate thy performance unto thee, that thy performance may be for the welfare of thy soul (2 Nephi 32:9).

But this is not all; they had given themselves to much prayer, and fasting; therefore they had the spirit of prophecy, and the spirit of revelation, and when they taught, they taught with power and authority of God (Alma 17:3).

Pray in your families unto the Father, always in my name, that your wives and your children may be blessed (3 Nephi 18:21).

The scriptures, quoting prophets, apostles, and especially the Savior have made it very clear that we should be praying regarding all things in our lives including our thanks, needs, and troubles.

Many of us were taught as children to pray at meals and at bedtime. Those are certainly opportune times to express our thanks and needs. However, the scriptures suggest that genuine prayer should have place in our hearts and minds, in fact all the time in all places we may be in (Alma 37:36-37).

> *But thou, when thou prayest, enter into thy closet, and when thou hast shut thy door, pray to thy Father which is in secret; and thy Father which seeth in secret shall reward thee openly* (Matthew 6:6).
> *But we will give ourselves continually to prayer* (Acts 6:4).
> *But behold, I say unto you that ye must pray always, and not faint* (2 Nephi 32:9).

Alma, instructing his son Helaman, prefaced his remarks which were reviewed earlier (Alma 37:36-37) with this counsel.

> *O, remember, my son, and learn wisdom in thy youth; yea, learn in thy youth to keep the commandments of God* (Alma 37:35).

This is wise counsel for all of us individually and for our families as we strive to follow the Savior, being encouraged to begin when we are young. Children and youth are capable and are filled with desire to have essential experiences, especially with prayer and the companionship of the Spirit, which prepares them for days to come.

This instruction regarding prayer encapsulates attitude, desire, effort, timing, and turning our hearts unto God with full purpose, full measure, being filled with thanksgiving for all of God's love and mercy in our behalf. What is promised? being lifted up at the last day, being worthy to return home to Father, to be in His presence and enjoy Eternal Life.

The Spirit knows what we should pray for, knowing the will of God (Romans 8:26). Inviting the Spirit to be our companion in prayer through our desire, effort, humility, and listening with full purpose of heart will provide the opportunity for the Spirit to inspire understanding regarding what we should pray for. This is essential to develop Christlike character.

Trusting God

Knowing that all things are in front of God, the past, present, and future, why is it that so many of God's children do not trust Him in all things relative to their lives?

> Trust in the Lord with all thine heart; and lean not unto thine own understanding. In all thy ways acknowledge him, and he shall direct thy paths (Proverbs 3:5-6).

This instruction was confirmed for me in an experience that came as a tender mercy and has provided a clarity of understanding and an increase of trust in God since that moment of this awakening. My wife and I were driving with some friends when the topic of conversation turned to a discussion of the financial success of people, individuals we each know. At that point, I mentally left the discussion. I didn't have the desire or the emotional energy to contribute. Frankly, I hurt. My work and business efforts were not very productive, financially. We were getting by, but it did not appear to me to be progressive. The comparison with those doing well with my situation, which had been going on for quite a while, was intimately painful, the shadow of failure feeling not far away.

As the conversation continued, I directed my attention to the passing landscape, and I tried to find relief by hiding within this new focus. My thoughts were random as I struggled until a whisper of the Spirit gained my full attention, both mind and heart. I was asked, "Don't you trust Me to get you where you need to be?" It was very clear that the Spirit had spoken. I knew that I needed to answer as plainly as possible. I did and that "spirit inquiry" has brought a blessing to my life that has strengthened and elevated my thoughts, hopes, faith, testimony and trust in the Lord.

It was evident to me then and now that Christ knows me and my needs. Christ will get us where we need to be if we will follow Him with full purpose of heart, yielding our hearts unto him.

The personal offering of trust to our Lord is not one we make now and again when it seems to suit our circumstances. Placing our trust in Him is a covenant that we must strive to keep every day of our lives.

> *O Lord, I have trusted in thee, and I will trust in thee forever. I will not put my trust in the arm of flesh; for I know that cursed is he that putteth his trust in the arm of flesh. Yea, cursed is he that putteth his trust in man or maketh flesh his arm* (2 Nephi 4:34).

> *Behold, God is my salvation, I will trust, and not be afraid; for the Lord JEHOVAH is my strength and my song; he also has become my salvation* (2 Nephi 22:2).

> *I say unto you, if ye have come to a **knowledge of the goodness of God**, and his **matchless power**, and his **wisdom**, and his **patience**, and his **long-suffering** towards the children of men; and also, the **atonement** which has been prepared from the foundation of the world, that thereby salvation might come to him that should **put his trust in the Lord**, and should be **diligent in keeping his commandments**, and **continue in the faith** even unto the end of his life, I mean the life of the mortal body—*

> *I say, that this is the man who receiveth salvation, through the atonement which was prepared from the foundation of the world for all mankind, which ever were since the fall of Adam, or who are, or who ever shall be, even unto the end of the world.*

> *And this is the means whereby salvation cometh. And there is none other salvation save this which hath been spoken of; neither are there any conditions whereby man can be saved except the conditions which I have told you* (Mosiah 4:6-8, emphasis added).

King Benjamin, in these three verses of scripture, beautifully describes the covenant we make in trusting God, and what God covenants we will receive, even salvation through the Atonement of Christ.

Trustworthy

When it comes to our relationship with Father and Jesus Christ, considering our mortal journey, what does it mean to be trustworthy? Even as it is vital for us to trust God, what value is that trust if we cannot be trusted? Is it possible to trust God and not be trustworthy? No! Trusting God requires the exercise of faith, commitment, and effort. What does being trustworthy require? Faith. Commitment. Effort. They are interrelated and cannot be separated.

Nephi, son of Helaman, as recorded in the Book of Mormon, gave up being the chief judge of the land, weary of the iniquity of his people. He determined *to preach the word of God all the remainder of his days* as did his brother Lehi (Helaman 5:4). Some years later it was recorded that Nephi was given the sealing power. The sealing power is the authority to bind an ordinance on earth and have it recognized eternally in the heavens. As he pondered the iniquities of his people, he heard a voice.

> *Blessed art thou, Nephi, for those things which thou hast done; for I have beheld how thou hast with unwearyingness declared the word which I have given unto thee, unto this people. And thou hast not feared them, and hast not sought thine own life, but has sought my will, and to keep my commandments.*
>
> *And now, because thou hast done this with such unwearyingness, behold, I will bless thee forever; and I will make thee mighty in word and in deed, in faith and in works; yea, even that all things shall be done unto thee according to thy word, for thou shalt not ask that which is contrary to my will* (Helaman 10:4-5).

This scripture clearly focuses on the relationship of Nephi with God and that trust and being trustworthy are interconnected, being part of each other.

There are other examples in the scriptures of being trustworthy and trusting. Samuel the Lamanite was charged by the Lord to preach to the Nephites in the land of Zarahemla. Samuel stood upon the walls of the city bearing witness and prophesying of the birth of Jesus Christ. Those who did not believe resorted to casting stones and shooting arrows at him, but he was not deterred by these actions. When he had completed the assignment the Lord gave him, he departed unhurt (Helaman 12-16). Trust and being trustworthy are clearly evident here.

The prophet Abinadi was sent by the Lord to King Noah and his subjects to bear witness of the iniquities of the king, his priests and the people. Abinadi did so, completing his mission under the threat of death. He was protected by the Spirit until he had born witness and prophesied of what would come unless the king and his people repented. They did not and Abinadi suffered death by fire (Mosiah 11-17). He trusted the Lord even under the threat of death and proved trustworthy until his mission was completed, requiring the sacrifice of his life as a witness to the king and his people.

Jesus Christ knew whose son He was and His mission in mortality. The requirements of that undertaking included the Atonement, which weighed heavily upon Him. With that impending burden He went to Gethsemane with His disciples.

And he went a little further, and fell on his face, and prayed, saying, O my Father, if it be possible, let this cup pass from me: nevertheless not as I will, but as thou wilt (Matthew 26:39).

It is impossible to fully appreciate that burden, nor what was required of the Savior in Gethsemane and on the cross as He completed the requirements of the Atonement. In this short verse we see trust and trustworthiness joined as one for the blessing of all of Father's children.

These examples are striking and perhaps appear more impressive than the situations we face in our lives, but ours are all important. We are to become saviors (D&C 103:9-10) for others and to do so we must gain Christlike character to fill the mission we have been given in mortality.

To become Christlike, we must trust God to get us where we need to be and take care of our needs, even as in these examples, as we express our trustworthiness by focusing on what we can do to be obedient and bless others. This requires a focus of desire, faith, gifts, and abilities, being attentive outside of ourselves in this labor. Or in other words, to live our lives following the example of the Savior striving to be filled with truth and light unto the blessing of others.

CHAPTER 21

━━━━ ∞•C⌒Ɔ•∞ ━━━━

BECOMING A SAINT

The Bible Dictionary, published by The Church of Jesus Christ of Latter-Day Saints, instructs that the word "saint" is the translation of a Greek word rendered as "holy" or "having been set apart for a sacred purpose." Over time, it came to be understood as "without blemish," as anything consecrated for God must be free of stain or imperfection. We know that Jesus Christ was without blemish, having committed no sin, a requirement to complete the Atonement.

In the New Testament, those who had covenanted to follow Jesus Christ and were baptized became known as saints. Yet, we know they were not without blemish, but people like us trying to find their way, hopefully Home. During the period of the apostasy, priesthood authority was withdrawn and much of the gospel was lost. The restoration of the Church of Jesus Christ reinstituted members being called saints. In fact, Joseph Smith was instructed by the Savior that the name of the Church should be The Church of Jesus Christ of Latter-Day Saints.

So, how is it that the former or latter-day members of Christ's church can be called saints according to this definition? The Savior's Church throughout history has called and instructed its members to provide service within the Church in many different capacities. In nearly all these calls or requests for service the members are "set apart" to fulfill the different calls and requirements. In all these calls authority to fulfill the responsibilities is given by the laying on of hands by those who have priesthood authority to formally set the person apart. All calls are given for sacred purposes, thus fulfilling the definition of "saint."

All calls or "settings apart" are to be exercised and fulfilled in love for God and His children. This love is sacred and emanates from Jesus Christ himself, the "pure love of Christ" or charity. This is a divine love and plan that everyone of God's children is encouraged to strive for by being faithful.

The design of mortality has within its foundation and the power of its existence the blessing of women and men in a multitude of ways, including instruction, the lifting of burdens, and the purifying power of God to sanctify or make holy those children who have determined to align their lives with the Savior as disciples.

Those who desire to progress to return Home will also be those who have sought and received the gift of charity and use it to determine how they will live from day to day. In a visitation with Jesus Christ, the prophet Moroni, said this to Him:

> *And now I know that this love which thou hast had for the children of men is charity; wherefore, except men shall have charity they cannot inherit that place which thou hast prepared in the mansions of thy Father* (Ether 12:34).

It is very clear that all of Father's children are required to seek, receive, and embrace charity, making it the operating focus of their lives. Supplanting negative emotions, thoughts, and desires, it will be a power that transforms who we are. Jesus Christ is the source of charity, and all saints must have it to be true disciples.

> *But charity is the pure love of Christ, and it endureth forever; and whoso is found possessed of it at the last day, it shall be well with him* (Moroni 7:47).

Whatever is of the world is temporary and will fail to deliver anything of eternal value. It seems reasonable to expect that saints (all those who have covenanted to follow Jesus Christ and have been baptized in His name) will embrace all the characteristics of charity and their actions will provide testimony of this fact.

> *And charity suffereth long, and is kind, and envieth not, and is not puffed up, seeketh not her own, is not easily provoked, thinketh no evil, and rejoiceth not in iniquity but rejoiceth in the truth, beareth all things, believeth all things, hopeth all things, endureth all things* (Moroni 7:45).

Let's examine each of these characteristics.

Suffereth long – suggests patience, self-control, tolerance and even forgiveness.

> *. . . but whosoever shall smite thee on thy right cheek, turn to him the other also* (Matthew 5:39).

Kind – gentle and helpful.

> *Therefore all things whatsoever ye would that men should do to you, do ye even so to them* (Matthew 7:12);
>
> *. . . do good to them that hate you, and pray for them which despitefully use you, and persecute you . . .* (Matthew 5:44).

Envieth not – not jealous.

> *And the Lord God hath commanded . . . that they should not envy . . .* (2 Nephi 26:32).

Not puffed up – not proud.

> *And whosoever shall exalt himself shall be abased; and he that shall humble himself shall be exalted* (Matthew 23:12).

And, O that ye would listen unto the word of his commands, and let not this pride of your hearts destroy your souls (Jacob 2:16)!

Seeketh not her own – is not self-serving, is focused outward and not inward.

Yea, and cry unto God for all thy support; yea, let all thy doings be unto the Lord, and withersoever thou goest let it be in the Lord; yea, let all thy thoughts be directed unto the Lord; yea, let the affections of thy heart be placed upon the Lord forever. Counsel with the Lord in all they doings . . . (Alma 37:36-37).

Not easily provoked – does not easily give way to anger or other negative responses.

Let all bitterness, and wrath, and anger, and clamour, and evil speaking, be put away from you, with all malice . . . (Ephesians 4:31).

Thinketh no evil – does not consider or embrace anything sinful or wicked.

For as he thinketh in his heart, so is he . . . (Proverbs 23:7).

Rejoiceth not in iniquity – to rejoice is to celebrate or find delight in; takes no pleasure or joy in anything sinful.

Rejoiceth not in iniquity, but rejoiceth in the truth (1 Corinthians 13:6).

Rejoiceth in the truth – celebrates and finds joy in truth.

Jesus saith unto him, I am the way, the truth, and the life: no man cometh unto the Father, but by me (John 14:6).

Beareth all things – accept, hold and support.

. . . Behold, here are the waters of Mormon (for thus were they called) and now, as ye are desirous to come into the fold of God,

and to be called his people, and are willing to bear one another's burdens, that they may be light;

Yea, and are willing to mourn with those that mourn; yea, and comfort those that stand in need of comfort, and to stand as witnesses of God at all times and in all things, and in all places that ye may be in, even until death, that ye may be redeemed of God, and be numbered with those of the first resurrection, that ye may have eternal life—

Now I say unto you, if this be the desire of your hearts, what have you against being baptized in the name of the Lord, as a witness before him that ye have entered into a covenant with him that ye will serve him and keep his commandments, that he may pour out his Spirit more abundantly upon you (Mosiah 18:8-10)?

Now when our hearts were depressed, and we were about to turn back, behold, the Lord comforted us, and said: Go amongst thy brethren, the Lamanites, and bear with patience thine afflictions, and I will give unto you success (Alma 26:27).

Wilt thou grant unto them that they may have strength, that they may bear their afflictions which shall come upon them because of the iniquities of this people (Alma 31:33).

These three scriptures highlight three of the many different ways "bearing all things" might be required by God in His service and focusing on the blessing of His children.

Believeth all things – when we are taught a truth and it is confirmed by the Spirit; we become responsible for it. That responsibility includes embracing it, making it part of our lives and sharing it when guided by the Spirit to do so. The Savior is the fountain or source of all truth. Consider the instruction contained in these scriptures about believing and embracing all truth.

Then said Jesus to those Jews which believed on him, If ye continue in my word, then are ye my disciples indeed;

And ye shall know the truth, and the truth shall make you free (John 8:31-32).

And truth is knowledge of things as they are, and as they were, and as they are to come (D&C 93:24).

And the arm of the Lord shall be revealed; and the day cometh that they who will not hear the voice of the Lord, neither the voice of his servants, neither give heed to the words of the prophets and apostles, shall be cut off among the people (D&C 1:14).

And whatsoever thing persuadeth men to do good is of me; for good cometh of none save it be of me. I am the same that leadeth men to all good; he that will not believe my words will not believe me-that I am; and he that will not believe me will not believe the Father who sent me. For behold, I am the Father, I am the light, and the life, and the truth of the world (Ether 4:12).

For you shall live by every word that proceedeth forth from the mouth of God.

For the word of the Lord is truth, and whatsoever is truth is light, and whatsoever is light is Spirit, even the Spirit of Jesus Christ (D&C 84:44-45).

<u>*Hopeth all things*</u> – unfailing confidence in righteousness.

And again, my beloved brethren, I would speak unto you concerning hope. How is it that ye can attain unto faith, save ye shall have hope?

And what is it that ye shall hope for? Behold I say unto you that ye shall have hope through the atonement of Christ and the power of his resurrection, to be raised unto life eternal, and this because of your faith in him according to the promise.

Wherefore, if a man have faith he must needs have hope; for without faith there cannot be any hope (Moroni 7:40-42).

This instruction from the prophet Moroni clearly explains that faith and hope are linked, and a person cannot have one without the other.

And now, I Moroni, would speak somewhat concerning these things; I would show unto the world that faith is things which are hoped for and not seen (Ether 12:6).

And now as I said concerning faith—faith is not to have a perfect knowledge of things; therefore if ye have faith ye hope for things which are not seen, which are true (Alma 32:21).

Alma and Moroni both explain that what is hoped for is not seen in order for it to be linked to faith. Alma adds one more clarification— what is hoped for must also be true. Therefore, our responsibility is to hope for all things that are true. How will we know? God will let us know. It will be through Christ's atonement and the Holy Ghost.

Endureth all things – to remain firm, to not give in to that which is challenging or unrighteous, to accept chastening and properly order life accordingly.

Blessed is the man that endureth temptation: for when he is tried, he shall receive the crown of life, which the Lord has promised to them that love him (James 1:12).

If ye endure chastening, God dealeth with you as with sons; for what son is he whom the father chasteneth not (Hebrews 12:7)?

Be patient in afflictions, for thou shalt have many; but endure them, for, lo, I am with thee, even unto the end of thy days (D&C 24:8, this revelation was given several months after the Church was organized and during intense persecution).

And blessed are they who shall seek to bring forth my Zion at that day, for they shall have the gift and the power of the Holy Ghost; and if they endure unto the end they shall be lifted up at the last day, and shall be saved in the everlasting kingdom of the Lamb (1 Nephi 13:37).

*Behold, I am the law, and the light. Look unto me, and
endure to the end, and ye shall live; for unto him that endureth
to the end will I give eternal life* (3 Nephi 15:9).

These scriptures reveal the specific need of faithful endurance when
tempted, as a result of God's chastening, and dealing with afflictions.
Those conditions will likely impact every soul in mortality. Even the
Savior dealt with temptation and afflictions. What is the result if we are
faithful in this? being "saved in the everlasting kingdom of the Lamb"
and receiving the blessing of Eternal Life!

If a person (saint) is found to possess these qualities of charity at the
last day,

> *. . . it shall be well with him.*
>
> *Wherefore, my beloved brethren, pray unto the Father with
> all the energy of heart, that ye may be filled with this love* (charity,
> the pure love of Christ), *which he hath bestowed upon all who
> are true followers of his Son, Jesus Christ; that ye may become the
> sons of God; that when he shall appear we shall be like him for we
> shall see him as he is; that we may have this hope; that we may be
> purified even as he is pure. Amen* (Moroni 7:47-48).

All these scriptures describe charity and the way the pure love of
Christ is used to bring about the Eternal Life of man. All saints and all
of God's children are to pray to Father for this gift and then have the
responsibility to use it to secure their place as faithful children of God
and to assist in His work.

If a person has been "set apart for a sacred purpose," what is the
work that is to be done? In the latter days, which are ours, we know that
people are formally set apart to perform all kinds of efforts within the
Savior's Church to bless the lives of others, work that ultimately helps to
lift the burdens of others, both temporal and spiritual. Is this the work
of saints? Absolutely!

Doing work that fulfills sacred purposes is certainly one of the essential elements that mortality was designed to contain. Mortal life permits and provides challenges, often difficult ones that meeting them faithfully will prepare all of God's children to come to know who they are, who He is, and to have an appreciation of this relationship. That knowledge only comes when the heart and mind are willing to recognize a greater power than themselves. This places the person in a position represented as being on one's knees, willing to be taught, and learn obedience from the God who gave them life and He who provided blessings by paying the price of the Atonement.

These experiences and challenges are designed to fill the soul with truth and light for God's children to choose to be faithful daughters and sons, worthy to receive the kind of life God has, Eternal Life.

Becoming holy can only happen through the Atonement of Jesus Christ. Atonement is an English word that when you break it into parts it looks like this, at-one-ment. Through the Atonement we can become one with Father and the Savior as we keep the covenants we have made. The covenants we make at baptism and reaffirm each time we take the sacrament qualify us to be known as saints. Our lives are also set aside through the saving ordinances of the Church and calls of service.

 Think about this. Say the name of the Church out loud as if you are bearing your testimony. The Church of Jesus Christ of Latter-Day Saints. There is power in the name for it bears witness of Jesus Christ and the blessings we can each have by being His disciple, a saint, having committed our lives to assist in God's work.

It is impossible to become a saint without the Savior's Atonement. We can't make ourselves holy. We can make covenants and strive our whole lives to keep them, but ultimately, holiness, perfection, or completeness is only possible through the Savior's sacrifice and the Atonement.

In His mercy and fulfillment of the work He was given, Jesus Christ offers us to "be perfected in Him" (Moroni 10:32-33). To do so we must follow the counsel of King Benjamin to "becometh as a child." King Benjamin's testimony makes it clear that we must respond to the *enticings of the Holy Spirit, and putteth off the natural man* (Mosiah 3:19) to become a saint and worthy to be perfected in Christ.

As imperfect as we are, if we are striving according to Moroni's instruction, we can, through God's covenant and grace be "perfect in Christ" and have a remission of our sins, becoming holy. As a result, an obvious choice must be made. Do you want to become one with God or one with the world? That is the choice we each must make. Following that decision are the myriads of choices that will be made in a lifetime to be worthy to be called a saint and return Home, filled with joy to be in Father's presence.

Do you rejoice in these words? Have you heard the voice of the Savior in these scriptures? Does your heart sing the song of redeeming love from our Father and His Only Begotten Son? If so, then it is incumbent upon us to submit to the will of Father to be worthy to return to Him, having met the requirements of becoming a "saint."

CHAPTER 22

—◦◦◦◦—

MEN ARE THAT THEY MIGHT HAVE JOY

Adam fell that men might be; and men are, that they might have joy (2 Nephi 2:25).

This instruction that the prophet Lehi gave to his son, Jacob, is one that should invite pondering and prayer on our part, perhaps throughout our lives. Remembering and trusting this inspired counsel will provide perspective even at difficult times. Do Father's children embrace this doctrine? Do you? Perhaps we all desire it, but life experiences often seem to have no happiness or joy in them.

Sometimes we may feel that joy is just a mirage. We can see it out there in the desert of our lives, but when we get to where it should be, it is not there. To some, life may seem mostly composed of stress, challenge, pain, confusion, even anger. Many people experience desperation, all the while looking for joy or something like it but rarely encounter it. These mortal responses do not seem to play any part in an experience of joy in life or because of life. They appear at times to be opposites.

As we work to meet the challenges that are in front of us from day-to-day, we might not recognize this liberating and joyful instruction from the prophet Lehi. Personal experience and reading the headlines of any daily newspaper might convince us that in no way is life designed to give us happiness. Oh sure, we get moments from time to time, but joy every day is not available or possible, or so it may seem. Some may say

165

that what the prophet has said makes a wonderful slogan or summary of life, but it isn't realistic.

Why then or how can a prophet of God, from thousands of years ago, say that the reason for our existence is "joy or happiness?" Have we been looking in all the wrong places? It is obvious that joy isn't something that we just happen upon or create out of our imagination. Joy or true happiness must be pursued on the appropriate path, anxiously meeting the required elements of that path. Lehi's instruction to Jacob, his son, is as follows confirming that *men are that they might have joy.*

> *And the Messiah cometh in the fulness of time, that he may redeem the children of men from the fall. And because that they are redeemed from the fall they have become free forever, knowing good from evil; to act for themselves and not to be acted upon, save it be by the punishment of the law at the great and last day, according to the commandments which God hath given* (2 Nephi 2:26).

Lehi then explains how joy is possible only *through the great Mediator of all men* (2 Nephi 2:27), which is Jesus Christ. To say it another way, Jesus Christ is the source of joy. Lehi bore witness that because of the redemption of men from Adam's fall men become free, understanding the difference between good and evil. Men have the blessing of choosing and Lehi makes it clear that either *liberty and eternal life* or *captivity and death* can be chosen by Father's children. Here are his instructions:

> *Wherefore, men are free according to the flesh; and all things are given them which are expedient unto man. And they are free to choose liberty and eternal life, through the great Mediator of all men, or to choose captivity and death, according to the captivity and power of the devil; for he seeketh that all men might be miserable like unto himself* (2 Nephi 2:27).

Before going further, why doesn't Father choose for us since we know He loves us? Wouldn't that provide the joy we all want? No, because true joy requires agency, the ability to make choices and receive rewards, either positive or negative, depending on our choices. Appreciating joy only occurs when we have experienced pain and sorrow, discovering in that process that we must expend the effort to be worthy to receive it. In support, Father has chosen for us by the counsel He gives, but not in the sense of Lucifer's offer, pre-mortally.

> *And I, the Lord God, spake unto Moses, saying: That Satan, whom thou hast commanded in the name of mine Only Begotten, is the same which was from the beginning, and he came before me, saying— Behold, here am I, send me, I will be they son, and I will redeem all mankind, that one soul shall not be lost, and surely I will do it; wherefore give me thine honor.*
>
> *But, behold, my Beloved Son, which was my Beloved and Chosen from the beginning, said unto me—Father, thy will be done, and the glory be thine forever.*
>
> *Wherefore, because that Satan rebelled against me, and sought to destroy the agency of man, which I, the Lord God, had given him, and also, that I should give unto him mine own power; by the power of mine Only Begotten, I caused that he should be cast down;*
>
> *And he became Satan, yea, even the devil, the father of all lies, to deceive and to blind men, and to lead them captive at his will, even as many as would not hearken unto my voice* (Moses 4:1-4).

Satan sought to force all of Father's children to Satan's desired end without giving them any option or agency to make their own choices. As can be determined from these scriptural verses, Father saw through Satan's attempt to destroy the agency of men and to acquire Father's power in this deceitful offer.

In preserving agency, the decisions of Father's children would be their own. The saving instruction and ordinances were put in place by Jesus Christ to invite all to use our agency to choose *liberty and eternal life*, but not by Godly decree. Yes, Father and the Savior do love us, so much so that their work is to convince us to follow Christ's example and learn the lessons leading to joy, to Eternal Life, to receive and appreciate the life Father has. This is the ultimate joy.

> *For behold, this is my work and my glory—to bring to pass*
> *the immortality and eternal life of man* (Moses 1:39).

Understanding that there is much of righteous desire and effort needed to become worthy to receive this ultimate joy, Eternal Life, we have not been left alone to determine what our spiritual relationship with Father and Christ should be. The Apostle Paul gave this instruction.

> *This I say then, Walk in the Spirit . . .*
> *. . . the fruit of the Spirit is love, joy, peace, longsuffering,*
> *gentleness, goodness, faith,*
> *Meekness, temperance . . .* (Galatians 5:16, 22- 23).

Paul understood the difference between "walking in the Spirit" with the fruits or outcomes of having the Spirit as our companion and being without it. Remember, he was a Pharisee and actively persecuted Christians, including taking part in the martyrdom of Stephen. He saw a vision of Jesus Christ and his life was changed. Paul knew very well the difference between having the Spirit in his life and not having it, the pain of sin and the joy of forgiveness.

His outline of the fruits of "walking with the Spirit" speaks invitingly and powerfully to being worthy of that companionship. True love and joy are companions; they cannot be separated as they are a part of each other. There are other emotions that may masquerade as true love, but they do not have the power, light, and longevity of love. For love lifts and refines when given the opportunity by the choices a person makes, and this is designed to be done on life's pathway.

How do those choices relate to the path that must be followed to receive them? Both prophetic comments identify the blessing of joy, and that Father wants to give it to all of His children, but they must be prepared, being worthy to receive it. It is a gift given by the Holy Ghost to those who search for and follow the covenant path. Joy isn't just something that some of Father's children will accidentally happen upon. It is the goal, the very reason for our existence, for all the inspiration, striving, sacrificing, work, and progression when embraced while in mortality, all correctly lead to joy and its receipt.

Joseph Smith's quote on gaining happiness has given additional information that helps to identify the correct life pathway that we must choose, and the progression required to receive joy. This pathway is an extension of the one we chose pre-mortally. It is a passageway that requires "virtue, uprightness, faithfulness, holiness, and keeping all the commandments of God." If we do so, true happiness or joy will be our reward, and that blessing is vastly different from the pleasure and periodic snatches of temporal happiness we might feel in the world outside of this path. They are not the same. True joy and love are so fundamental to the life Christ wants us to obtain, that when we do so, they do not disappear when challenges come.

Can you imagine walking the path that leads to joy and not loving Jesus Christ with all your heart and soul? Lehi's instruction, 2 Nephi 2:25-27, which we reviewed earlier, is a wonderful summary of the role of mortality in the development of love, loyalty, righteousness, and the battle that is taking place right now for the souls of Father's children.

Many souls may not realize that there is a battle taking place and powerful opposition to our receiving the blessings of love, joy and Eternal Life. These gifts fortify our faithful decisions and give us strength and determination to turn away from the adversary's efforts of deceit and corruption. Satan may try to duplicate these wonderful gifts, but he cannot. He can only imitate. What is advertised by him is not the real thing, only a poor artificial attemp that cannot produce what is claimed. His opposition will be turned to blessing for us as we maintain our loyalty to Christ.

> *For it must needs be, that there is an opposition in all things. If not so, my firstborn in the wilderness, righteousness could not be brought to pass, neither wickedness, neither holiness nor misery, neither good nor bad* (2 Nephi 2:11).

Christ uses this opposition as part of the process to obtaining joy. Even in opposition there is great blessing, or especially because of opposition. Think of what is required to meet it successfully. One must gain strength and understanding, exercise faith and hope, experience conversion, and ultimately receive the refining of our souls. Keep in mind that receiving all these blessings is conditional on our choices. Freedom of choice is essential to joy.

If we are not free to choose, then we are in bondage.

> *For as many as are led by the Spirit of God, they are the sons* (and daughters) *of God.*
>
> *For ye have not received the **spirit of bondage** again to fear; but ye have received the **Spirit of adoption**, whereby we cry, Abba, Father* (Romans 8:14-15, emphasis added).

Paul's instruction from Romans bears witness that *we have not received the spirit of bondage,* but are saved by receiving *the spirit of adoption,* by recognizing who is our Father and the blessings inherit in that relationship as he confirms that we have been accepted His children. However, we can by our choices take the steps to place ourselves in bondage to the adversary of all that is good.

What is the spirit of bondage? When a person is in bondage they are controlled by some kind of compulsive force, which does not permit the person to make their own choices. We have seen throughout mortal history many peoples and nations come under bondage to a superior physical force. This is one possibility leading to bondage and there are others.

Many of us may have some experience with addiction, a compelling force in our beings that may affect us physically and/or emotionally. With addiction, we have given up the ability to make choices in those areas of life that the addiction affects such as with drugs and our physical needs and behaviors.

Addiction can cause us to be compulsive, affecting our emotions and reasoning. Gambling is one such source of bondage that doesn't begin with the physical being. Physical and emotional bondage also negatively impact our spirituality and ability to align our lives with Christ's desires for us and to receive His help with our personal challenges. Being out of control, how do we go about recovering and realigning ourselves with healthy principles and actions?

The easy answer is don't start down that road, but that may not be very helpful considering where you are in life. Let's examine how bondage ultimately takes control of our lives. Some folks will take a "test drive" with something they are considering. Their reasoning is that it may or may not be good for them, but what can a test drive hurt? If I don't like it or I determine it isn't good for me, I will figure that out, and I won't do it anymore. With that promise to ourselves, we go forward doing exactly what Satan wants us to do.

"Just try this a little bit. It won't hurt you," Satan whispers to us. So, some do try it. The temptation that encouraged us to do what our conscience said wasn't a good idea, well, it wins out. It doesn't matter if it is a drug or a questionable act. The next step in addiction comes more naturally as we have already permitted Satan to influence our decisions. If we allow his encouragement to take us there, he has us where he wants us. Multiple "experiments" or experiences will lead us to bondage and then what do we do?

Remember, Satan is in no hurry. He has been perfecting his evil craft since the creation of the world. He will come again and again to test your resolve. It makes sense to declare your love, affinity, repentance and commitment to Jesus Christ and His gospel daily. By doing so, you invite the Spirit to be your companion and the receipt of the power and blessing that Christ can give to protect and advance you in life.

Each child of Father has been given the Light of Christ or a conscience. This gift is designed and filled with divine purpose to turn us to the Savior with full purpose of heart and to prepare us to receive the Gift of the Holy Ghost, a companion representing the Godhead with power to guide our lives in righteousness.

True joy is conditional upon our relationship with Jesus Christ. Ponder upon what he said to his disciples about this relationship.

> *As the Father hath loved me, so have I loved you: continue ye in my love.*
>
> ***If ye keep my commandments, ye shall abide in my love;*** *even as I have kept my Father's commandments, and abide in his love.*
>
> *These things have I spoken unto you, that my joy might remain in you, and **that your joy might be full*** (John 15:9-11, emphasis added).

We abide in the Savior's love by keeping His commandments. If we do so, we will be blessed with a fullness of joy.

What if we have taken steps down the road that will never provide joy? If we don't turn around, corruption and destruction await, according to Satan's plan. It is not too late to change direction. We do so by humbly turning to Christ and striving with all the energy and desire we can muster to turn from sin and repent, genuinely desiring to change our lives. Repentance is a choice. If we desire it, heavenly help will be given.

> *And no unclean thing can enter into his* (Father's) *kingdom; therefore nothing entereth into his rest save it be those who have washed their garments in my blood, because of their faith, and the repentance of all their sins, and their faithfulness unto the end* (3 Nephi 27:19).

Therefore, repent all ye ends of the earth, and come unto me, and believe in my gospel, and be baptized in my name; for he that believeth and is baptized shall be saved; but he that believeth not shall be damned; and signs shall follow them that believe in my name.

And blessed is he that is found faithful unto my name at the last day, for he shall be lifted up to dwell in the kingdom prepared for him from the foundation of the world (Ether 4:18-19).

Behold, he who has repented of his sins, the same is forgiven, and I, the Lord, remember them no more (D&C 58:42).

Our Father knew that His children would make mistakes, poor choices, even commit rebellion, and yet He provided the way to be cleansed from destruction, from sin through the Atonement of Jesus Christ. The plan Father has for His children is a plan designed for their preparation to receive true joy, the joy that all will receive if worthy to dwell in His presence.

And if men come unto me I will show unto them their weakness. I give unto men weakness that they may be humble; and my grace is sufficient for all men that humble themselves before me; for if they humble themselves before me, and have faith in me, then will I make weak things become strong unto them (Ether 12:27)

Within this instruction from the Lord, we gain understanding of the role of challenges and weaknesses, all designed for our development and the receipt of strength, ability, and understanding to provide instruction for the worthiness necessary to return Home.

In a very focused commandment, the Savior put all things in proper perspective.

Thou shalt thank the Lord they God in all things (D&C 59:7).

173

If we love Jesus Christ and exercise faith in Him; trusting Him to guide our steps, to protect our being, to get us where we need to be, even the challenges of opposition can be turned to strengthen us and used to bring about the blessings needed in our lives. Believe Him. Love Him. Trust Him. Follow Him.

And if ye do always remember me ye shall have my Spirit to be with you (3 Nephi 18:11).

Joy will be the definitive reward.

CHAPTER 23

—◦◦◦◦—

LOVE IS IRREPLACEABLE

W hen we experience true love, love which is of a divine source, no other emotion, feeling, delight, or attraction is capable of taking its place. It doesn't matter what the others are, they do not have the refining ability or support the binding influence and power needed to fill the soul with joy. This love provides incentive to make changes even when facing the most difficult of challenges that threaten fear and trepidation. True love is more powerful than they all. Love emanates from Father and Christ. That is its origin. It begins with Them. We make place for it in our lives when we are striving to align our lives with the Savior by our obedience and striving to love as He loves.

> *The scriptures are laid before thee, yea, and all things denote there is a God; yea, even the earth, and all things that are upon the face of it, yea, and its motion, yea, and also all the planets which move in their regular form do witness that there is a Supreme Creator* (Alma 30:44).

This is the testimony that Alma bore to Korihor, who claimed that there is no god. Alma's witness is that *all things* bear testimony that there is a *Supreme Creator*. All things also bear witness of Father's and Christ's love for all of us. For why was there a creation if not for the love and blessing of all of Father's children? We know from other scripture that God's work and glory is to bring to pass the immortality of His children and the blessing of Eternal Life (Moses 1:39). Are these gifts of love? Absolutely. All things bear this witness.

The focus on love and its attributes is found throughout this manuscript and the scriptures cited. It is impossible to live a righteous life without love. It is part of and on display in every particle, experience, instruction, or operation of our world, solar system, and universe. The signature of God's love is upon all His creations.

For our reception of the gifts of creation, of life and love, God has asked that we trust Him, align our lives with Him, and keep His commandments. His desire for us is to progress in our development to become like Him. For these blessings which are inherited in our progressive mortal walk, we haven't been required to complete some great difficult act or service that would be seen in mortality as overwhelming or nearly impossible. We are required to learn of Christ, then follow Him. Here are His words of invitation.

> *Come unto me, all ye that labour and are heavy laden, and I will give you rest.*
>
> *Take my yoke upon you, and* **learn of me***; for I am meek and lowly in heart: and ye shall find rest unto your souls.,*
>
> *For my yoke is easy, and my burden is light* (Matthew 11:28-30, emphasis added).

We are to learn of Him and take His yoke upon us. When we are baptized, we take upon us His name and promise to keep His commandments. We make that promise again every time we partake of the sacrament. This promise is a covenant with Christ that when kept secures our relationship with Him. The burden is light. It is easy to carry if we are true to our covenant to be faithful and strive to keep the commandments. If we do so, we have the promise that we *shall find rest unto* our souls. There is no outcome the world can produce equal to this promise.

This burden, taking upon us His yoke, is designed to be borne by all of Father's children, having many different abilities, personal challenges and backgrounds. We have each been given a wonderful gift to assist us, the Light of Christ. Those who have taken upon them this yoke will be blessed with truth and a "lighted pathway" bringing them to Christ's church and receipt of baptism and the Gift of the Holy Ghost.

This covenant pathway will lead us to Christ's presence and our return Home, that we may have the same quality of life He has. Knowing this, it is easier to understand why we must keep the commandments. When we make them a part of our lives, striving to be consistent in our efforts, we will find our lives, our abilities and desires, refined and strengthened by them. Christ ordered these redemptive requirements and values into two great commandments.

> *. . . Thou shalt love the Lord thy God with all thy heart, and with all thy soul, and with all thy mind.*
> *This is the first and great commandment.*
> *And the second is like unto it, Thou shalt love thy neighbour as thyself* (Matthew 22:37-39).

With an understanding of how important our loyalty to Christ is, and working every day to keep the commandments, this instruction from King Benjamin puts Christ's love and gifts in perspective.

> *I say unto you that if ye should serve him who has created you from the beginning, and is preserving you from day to day, by lending you breath, that ye may live and move and do according to your own will, and even supporting you from one moment to another—I say, if ye should serve him with all you whole souls yet ye would be unprofitable servants* (Mosiah 2:21).

King Benjamin's use of *lending you breath* rather than giving or supplying it suggests that there is a requirement to return what has been loaned to us. Father owns all things. It includes everything we have received from the creation of the world and from our own creation.

> *And behold, all that he requires of you is to keep his commandments; and he has promised you that if ye would keep his commandments ye should prosper in the land; and he never doth vary from that which he hath said, therefore, if ye do keep his commandments he doth bless you and prosper you.*
>
> *And now, in the first place, he hath created you, and granted unto you your lives, for which ye are indebted unto him.*
>
> *And secondly, he doth require that ye should do as he hath commanded you; for which if ye do, he doth immediately bless you; and therefore he hath paid you. And ye are still indebted unto him, and are, and will be forever and ever; therefore, of what have ye to boast (Mosiah 2:22-24)?*

And what are we to return to Him? Us, having used the creations as Christ intended, having accepted and embraced Godly love for our education, progression and transformation. Mortality was given and breath loaned for these purposes and we will always be in debt to God. Is not this a witness of the power of love?

Perhaps there is in the back of our minds, as we ponder upon our relationship with the Savior, concern about all the truly challenging experiences we have in life? These may not feel like they are evidence of Godly love. God made it very clear to Joseph Smith that adversity, even painful difficulties that may have seemed beyond his abilities, are a part of life and will be turned to blessing as he exercises faith in God's love and works.

> *My son, peace be unto thy soul; thine adversity and thine afflictions shall be but a small moment;*

And then, if thou endure it well God shall exalt thee on high; thou shalt triumph over all thy foes (D&C 121:7-8).

This same promise is made to all of God's children. It is fundamental to our relationship with Christ, and to the gospel, which has been given to encourage and guide in preparing us to receive all that Father has prepared for His children. This is continuing evidence of His love. We each must endure well the challenges that come in mortality. They are an integral part of it, providing the objects of desire and will do so for the exercise of faith unto the receiving of God's blessings. We cannot mature and become an heir to all that Father has unless we learn to overcome difficulty and challenge. Education, hands-on education, is essential.

> *The Spirit itself beareth witness with our spirit, that we are the children of God:*
>
> *And if children, then heirs; heirs of God, and joint-heirs with Christ; if so be that we suffer with him, that we may be also glorified together* (Romans 8:16-17).
>
> *Behold I say unto you, that whosoever has heard the words of the prophets, yea, all the holy prophets who have prophesied concerning the coming of the Lord—I say unto you, that all those who have hearkened unto their words, and believed that the Lord would redeem his people, and have looked forward to that day for a remission of their sins, I say unto you, that these are his seed, or they are the heirs of the kingdom of God* (Mosiah 15:11).

Paul and Abinadi, on different continents and at different times, bore witness that the design of mortality for all of Father's children is to prepare them to become heirs of His kingdom. The obedience required is that they will heed and follow the words of the prophets, exercising faith in Jesus Christ and the power of His redemption for all of Father's faithful children.

We have many advocates but only have one real foe. Satan is a determined adversary. However, the promise is in place for each of God's children that if they will receive His love with thanksgiving and return it to Him and give love to all of Father's children on the earth, we will receive the rewards of faithfulness as a true heir of celestial blessing.

> *Let thy bowels also be full of charity towards all men, and to the household of faith, and let virtue garnish they thoughts unceasingly; then shall thy confidence wax strong in the presence of God; and the doctrine of the priesthood shall distil upon thy soul as the dews from heaven.*
>
> *The Holy Ghost shall be thy constant companion, and thy scepter an unchanging scepter of righteousness and truth; and thy dominion shall be an everlasting dominion and without compulsory means it shall flow unto thee forever and ever* (D&C 121:45-46).

To be full of charity is to be filled with pure love, loving as Christ loves and to love Him with that same love. It is irreplaceable. The blessings that come from the exercise of this love have power to reshape and refine our lives, facilitating our progression to become more like Jesus Christ.

> *For he that receiveth my servants receiveth me* (Christ);
> *And he that receiveth me receiveth my Father;*
> *And he that receiveth my Father receiveth my Father's kingdom; therefore all that my Father hath shall be given unto him* (D&C 84:36-39).

To receive all that Father has is to become an heir and to receive the love and blessing of our Parent. The love of our parents in mortality is a shadow of Father's love for all His children and His desire to bless their lives, even as we desire to bless our children.

We have earlier reviewed this scripture, but its application to this discussion of what is required to be an heir and the blessings that will accompany our progression is a tender and awe-inspiring observation.

> *Wherefore, my beloved brethren, I know that if ye shall follow the Son, with full purpose of heart, acting no hypocrisy and no deception before God, but with real intent, repenting of your sins, witnessing unto the Father that ye are willing to take upon you the name of Christ, by baptism—yea, by following your Lord and your Savior down into the water, according to his word, behold, then shall ye receive the Holy Ghost; yea, then cometh the baptism of fire and of the Holy Ghost; and then can ye speak with the tongue of angels and shout praises unto the Holy One of Israel* (2 Nephi 31:13).

This instruction from Nephi explains what we must do to receive Christ and this is the required step to receive all the blessings He has reserved for us. Do you desire to *speak with the tongue of angels and shout praises unto the Holy One of Israel?* That will be your desire if you follow the instructions from these prophets, loving as we are loved by Father and Jesus Christ.

Love or charity is a power of eternal progression and a shield against the adversary's attempts at destruction. It is the repository for righteous desire, effort and sacrifice, totally unaffected by distance and time, a power that changes lives and awakens our souls to who we are.

CHAPTER 24

—◦◦◦◦◦—

MANNA

At the time of the exodus of the Children of Israel from Egypt, it is estimated that this "freed nation" was composed of approximately two million individuals, men, women, and children. The people had been captives and slaves in Egypt for about 400 years. This meant that generations lived and died under the culture of slavery and their thoughts and understanding of the components of life were undoubtedly greatly impacted by these circumstances, including the passage of time.

When Moses led them from Egypt, likely there were some who did not possess the attitudes and abilities that a free people would normally have in supporting themselves from day to day. Perhaps many did not have the robust mental and spiritual strengths that free people would have, because of life experiences. Personal experiences and legacy understanding passed down through generations are blessings that provide guidance in decision-making and day-to-day living requirements.

To say it in another way, they may not have possessed the learned abilities to now make choices and provide for themselves in a state of self-determination with all the options that would become available to them. There was much they had to learn and accomplish. Being children of a loving God, they would begin this necessary required education with changes of lifestyle and progression that would immediately impact their lives now and for future generations.

With a change of location, the first of their needs that had to be addressed was what food would be available to them? Any food they were able to take with them would disappear quickly. What was to be done to handle this daily need?

Feeding two million people was a problem that their leadership must have felt keenly and with great concern. The Lord in His wisdom and kindness provided food that resolved the pangs of hunger—manna (which in Hebrew means, What is it?) and became known as "heaven sent bread." The Lord told Moses; *I will rain bread from heaven for you* (Exodus 16:4). Following the disappearance of dew each morning, the manna appeared and had a flake-like shape, tasting like a wafer with honey. It disappeared under the heat of the sun and would spoil by the next day if they tried to store it.

This daily event of heaven-sent-food was a miracle for physical sustenance with the nutrition needed for good health (Exodus 16:4-31).

> *. . . put your trust in God . . . that God who brought the children of Isreal out of the land of Egypt*
> *. . . and fed them with manna that they might not perish in the wilderness, and many more things did he do for them* (Mosiah 7:19).

Why did God do it? Because He loved them and wanted to bless them. They are His children. There were requirements in using the manna and an important one was that it could not be stored from one day to the next. It spoiled before the new day arrived.

I wonder how this requirement affected the people, especially in the beginning. Would they be fearful that it would end, as this was something they could not physically control and use according to their own desires? They were totally dependent upon God to provide for their needs. Their only option outside of finding their own food was the exercise of faith, bridging one day to the next. However, manna was not sent on the Sabbath, but could be stored from the day before without spoiling, a miracle witness of the sanctity of this day.

On the first day manna was provided, I'm certain that the people rejoiced in this gift, even as they were given to wonder about it. Would this tender mercy invite the investment of obedience and the exercise of faith for the next day and the next? Would the people just hope the miracle would continue without meeting the spiritual requirement that is so apparent to us today, the exercise of faith?

Recognizing the immense challenge of procuring food every day for 2,000,000 people, providing daily guidance on how they should act and encouraging the development of trust in the Lord that their needs would be met, was the challenge that faced them and their leaders. Would they genuinely face it with faith? Did they recognize the evidence of love in this gift? Did the immensity of the challenge drive them to their knees? Would it do so for you?

In God's tender mercy, hunger was satisfied for only a day, except for the Sabbath, and the exercise of trust was required from one day to the next. How would we respond if our ability to put food on the table was good for only a day? To trust in God's help daily and to receive that which is needed for the blessing of our lives is no different for us today than it was for them in the exercise of faith.

The gift of manna with the requirements for its use inspired development and progression in both the temporal and spiritual needs of the individual. The exercise of faith to receive and the wise use for physical needs inspired growth in these two essential parts of a person.

Manna became a symbol of God's love and care for His children. The miracle of its appearing and the instructions for its use provided a clear testimony that God wanted a relationship that was recognized and embraced daily, as fully as possible.

Is it any different for us today? Does God want a daily relationship with us? Where is the manna that we need? Will it be given to us? Has it been given, if so, why don't we recognize, accept, and embrace it? Our needs are really no different than those of the Children of Israel. So, what do we have in our lives that serves as manna for us and provides blessing as it did for them?

Perhaps you will have additional items from those listed here to add to the possible components of manna. Remember, manna was created to provide daily nourishment, spiritually and physically.

1. Light of Christ
2. Gift of the Holy Ghost
3. Prayer
4. Church attendance
5. Calls to service
6. Sacrificing time and resources to bless others

We may not have the necessity of securing daily food in front of us, but what challenges are in front of you day-to-day, often producing unrelenting pressure on your family and you? Do you find the need for the constant application of faith to guide you as these people must have felt? The miracle of conversion to truth, to the gospel, requires the refining of our souls and is the requisite goal to inspire commitment and the exercise of strength from day to day. It is real. Perhaps you may feel some kinship with the Children of Israel as you face challenges that you can't control and must exercise faith sufficient for the blessings needed. Do you rejoice in the "manna" that has been gifted to you?

The challenges in our day are as significant as were those the Children of Israel faced on their pathway to a promised land, as we follow a covenant path that we have not traveled before. The trials of maintaining a faithful relationship with the Savior and meeting the requirements of our pathway progression will likely require the stretching of our souls, stamina, growth in strength, ability, desire, and trust. I have to admit I am thankful that I don't have the challenge of finding daily food for my family.

However, I have other challenges that require the exercise of faith and trust daily for me to fulfill my stewardships. If the Israelites knew about the tests of our time, do you think they would be thankful that they didn't have to meet them? We live in a fallen world and the forces of evil seem to be gathering strength and growing all around us.

The Savior answered the question about the manna and our needs as recorded in the Book of John while teaching those that followed him near the Sea of Galilee.

> *They said therefore unto him, What sign shewest thou then, that we may see, and believe thee? What dost thou work?*
>
> *Our fathers did eat manna in the desert; as it is written, He gave them bread from heaven to eat.*
>
> *Then Jesus said unto them, Verily, verily, I say unto you, Moses gave you not that bread from heaven; but* **my Father giveth you the true bread from heaven.**
>
> **For the bread of God is he which cometh down from heaven and giveth life unto the world.**
>
> *Then said they unto him, Lord, evermore give us this bread.*
>
> **And Jesus said unto them, I am the bread of life: he that cometh to me shall never hunger; and he that believeth on me shall never thirst.**
>
> **Verily, verily, I say unto you, He that believeth on me hath everlasting life.**
>
> **I am that bread of life.**
>
> *Your fathers did eat manna in the wilderness, and are dead.*
>
> *This is the bread which cometh down from heaven, that a man may eat thereof, and not die.*
>
> **I am the living bread which came down from heaven:** *if any man eat of this bread, he shall live for ever: and the bread that I will give is my flesh, which I will give for the life of the world* (John 6:30-35, 47-51, emphasis added).

The Savior, as God of the Old Testament, gave the Children of Israel manna to sustain their mortal lives and provide instruction and experiences that were needed for the sanctification of their souls. Manna is symbolic of the *living bread,* the *bread of life* given from heaven, which is Jesus Christ. He made the gift and sacrifice of His life so that all would receive immortality and have the opportunity, if faithful, to receive the blessing of Eternal Life. The gift of His life and meeting the requirements of sacrifice for the completion of the Atonement was essential.

As we make our way through the "wilderness" of mortality, there are other gifts from God that are representative of the spirit of manna and provide for our daily needs such as: scriptures, living prophets, daily blessing that supports our families both physically and spiritually. Perhaps you are one of those "children" who feel that General Conference every six months is truly "bread from heaven."

We are the brothers and sisters of the Children of Israel, and they were led on the path to a promised land. We are receiving from God the daily blessings needed for the aligning of our lives with His will, both spiritual and physical, to travel on the covenant path to lands of promise.

As with manna, our daily spiritual health requires us to receive and embrace the heavenly gifts we receive, as if consuming food, while striving to receive the offered vital relationship with Jesus Christ, *the living bread which came down from heaven.* Manna was a gift of love then, even as it is now. Christ is the manna, *the bread of life.* We consume Him like manna when we partake of the emblems of the sacrament.

CHAPTER 25

JOINING PETER, A DISCIPLE OF CHRIST

*Go ye therefore, and teach all nations, baptizing them in the
name of the Father, and of the Son, and of the Holy Ghost:*

*Teaching them to observe all things whatsoever I have
commanded you: and, lo, I am with you alway, even unto the
end of the world. Amen* (Matthew 28:19-20).

This is the instruction that Christ gave His apostles following
His resurrection. They were to spread the gospel throughout
the world to all nations, baptizing those who received and
acted upon the truth, becoming new disciples of the Lord.

According to the Bible Dictionary, (published by the Church of Jesus
Christ of Latter-Day Saints) a disciple is "a pupil or learner; a name used
to denote (1) the Twelve, also called Apostles, (2) all followers of Jesus
Christ." The need to always be learning from our mortal experiences
and from the guidance given so freely by the Spirit when we are willing
to receive, is fundamental in being a disciple of Jesus Christ.

And what are disciples supposed to be doing? In the Sermon on the
Mount, Christ gave this instruction.

Let your light so shine before men, that they may see your good works, and glorify your Father which is in heaven (Matthew 5:16).

Disciples are to live the teachings, the gospel of Jesus Christ, at all times and in all places. If they do so, their very presence will affect those who watch and receive them, as the faithful will be imbued with a light that is discernable to the spirit of each of us, a light that bears witness of truth and Jesus Christ. Remember, Christ is the source of all truth and light.

Becoming a disciple of Christ should be the goal of all of us, even as it was for Peter. The Savior gave some instructions, as recorded by Matthew in the New Testament, of what is required to be His disciple.

He that loveth father or mother more than me is not worthy of me: and he that loveth son or daughter more than me is not worthy of me.

And he that taketh not his cross, and followeth after me, is not worthy of me.

He that findeth his life shall lose it: and he that loseth his life for my sake shall find it (Matthew 10:37-39).

To some this instruction might seem harsh or confusing, but let's examine it more closely. Certainly, Father and the Savior want us to love and honor our parents (Exodus 20:12), our children, all our relatives and neighbors. There are commandments in place regarding the exercise of this true love. We must not forget that Jesus Christ is the source of love. Not one of us "children" is a source as the Savior is. It begins and flows from Him. We may embrace it and make it a part of our being, reflect it to others, hopefully adding our own love.

If we love Him, more than anyone or anything else, our relationship with Him and the blessings He gives will align our lives with family members and others in exactly the right relationships.

189

Taking upon us our "cross" is to receive whatever happens in life, the challenges, the trials, the pains and sorrows, trusting the Savior to give us strength and help to lift our burdens, as we give Him our loyalty. Our faith will be perfected, and our works aligned with Christ, trusting Him to guide our steps, no matter what we are experiencing as we walk the covenant path.

Alma, upon leaving his place as one of King Noah's priests, having been converted by Abinadi's instruction and witness of truth, went about teaching the gospel in private (Mosiah 12-18). His instruction at the waters of Mormon to those who were converted through his preaching and preparing for baptism, examined what it means to be baptized and to be a disciple of Jesus Christ, thereby coming into the *fold of God*. His testimony compliments Matthew's and Nephi's instruction.

> *And it came to pass that he said unto them: Behold, here are the waters of Mormon (for thus were they called) and now, as ye are desirous to come into the fold of God, and to be called his people, and are willing to bear one another's burdens, that they may be light;*
>
> *Yea, and are willing to mourn with those that mourn; yea, and comfort those that stand in need of comfort, and to stand as witnesses of God at all times and in all things, and in all places that ye may be in, even until death, that ye may be redeemed of God, and be numbered with those of the first resurrection, that ye may have eternal life—*
>
> *Now I say unto you, if this be the desire of your hearts, what have you against being baptized in the name of the Lord, as a witness before him that ye have entered into a covenant with him, that ye will serve him and keep his commandments, that he may pour out his Spirit more abundantly upon you* (Mosiah 18:8-10)?

These prophets have written with clarity and power, sufficiently that our hearts and minds will be awakened to these truths, if we exercise the desire to receive the Spirit, to be taught, and then align our lives according to the truth and light that will be given. Is there anyone who would not be blessed and experience a remarkable change of life by serving God and keeping His commandments, *that he may pour out his Spirit more abundantly upon you?* None!

When we live our lives in obedience to Christ's instruction and in service to Him, we give up that which is temporary in this world and receive the components that will refine and purify our lives, preparing us to use the heavenly gifts given to complete our mortal mission. If we give all that we have in faith and lose our lives in being a true disciple of Jesus Christ, He will give us all that Father has set aside for our blessing, even Eternal Life. Christ said,

> *Behold, I am the law, and the light. Look unto me, and endure to the end, and ye shall live; for unto him that endureth to the end will I give eternal life* (3 Nephi 15:9).

Peter knew that the promise, the covenant he had made to Jesus Christ, was to give Him his life and all the abilities he had to "feed the Savior's sheep." It became evident to Peter and should become so to us, that we cannot "lose our lives" and "feed the Savior's sheep," unless we love Him as He loves us. *Lovest thou me more than these* (John 21:15)?

CHAPTER 26

⋙∘⦇⟆∘⦈∘⋘

DISCIPLESHIP AND THE
REFINING OF OUR SOULS

It is imperative in becoming a disciple of Jesus Christ, to know who He is, His lineage, power and the responsibility He has in completing the work of salvation for all of Father's children. To delineate all that He brings to these responsibilities from our premortal lives to the experience of mortality and the completion of the salvation process is impossible in this work or in any other work, no matter how large or encompassing. To record all of the life, responsibility and work of Jeus Christ would require libraries and efforts beyond mortal ability.

Thankfully, divine revelation has been given that in brevity provides the foundation needed for each of Father's children to receive and embrace personal confirmation and understanding sufficient to give each of us the ability to become "true disciples." The implication and application of discipleship requires us to not only begin to know Him, but to follow Him by aligning our lives with His. Performing the work that we are and will become capable of in blessing the lives of others, having Christ as our embraced example, is all part of discipleship. In following Him, we are to become saviors, blessing and lifting the burdens of others, assisting in travel along the temporal pathway of each of us (D&C 103:9).

We have Heavenly Parents. Christ's Father is our Father. The qualities of Godliness were experienced in that Heavenly Home before coming to earth. We know from scripture that we were instructed, guided, led by Christ and others to prepare us for the next phase in our development, mortal life with a physical body.

Here, we are required to find our way, having been prepared for the mortal journey earlier, but without memory of all our experiences in that sacred Home. Not remembering does not change who we are, what we learned, or what our eternal goals are. It does require us to learn, resolve, change, refine, and be converted to truth. This happens through the active requirements and actions that have the potential to restore, refine, and preserve that which will draw us nearer to Christ. Receiving the rewards that faithful children receive through striving to return to the Home of our Parents is certainly the goal.

Pondering, desiring, searching, and coming to understand why this life process must be this way is an important component of our education and is certainly essential to our progression. There is no question that we all are members of the Family of Man. We may have different interests, talents, and Godly gifts from each other, and yet many of the gifts are comparable or have similar potential to produce the needed results. Our experiences with the Holy Ghost may vary from one person to another being designed for our specific needs, but the intent of all promptings, instruction, and experiences will be to refine who we are and guide us in drawing nearer to Jesus Christ while truly taking upon us His name.

Some of these experiences will be difficult, perhaps even painful physically, emotionally, and or spiritually. Similarities with other people will help to draw us together and differences will assist us in recognizing that each child of Father is unique and capable of inspiring wonder and appreciation, providing blessing in ways we might not have imagined. As we progress, love will blossom and fill our souls with appreciation and love for each other. We may not agree with the choices of others or understand what they are doing with their lives, but that is no hinderance to the exercise of love. Perspective will invite thanksgiving for abilities and strengths in others that may be weak within us. Is there anything that can prevent us from receiving these soul-stirring awakenings throughout life? Only our own biases, selfishness and attitudes.

Recently, I have been engaged in trying to understand and manage a situation, one that has the potential to be a blessing or a . . . misfortune. For simplicity purposes, the situation could be productive or a waste of personal resources. The true defining element is me. Here is how the situation has affected my psyche and emotions. I have felt joy that has brought peace and thanksgiving to my soul and in opposition, painful fear that felt as if it had surrounded my heart with tendrils designed to squeeze the life out of me. Perhaps you have had an experience like this in your life.

I sought comfort in the scriptures and prayer, as the resolve for this challenge is not immediately in front of me and may not be for a while. I examined the life and experiences of Jesus Christ, Peter and Paul, who became apostles to Christ, and Joseph Smith, the prophet through whom Jesus Christ restored His church in our modern era. The scriptures have revealed some remarkably interesting things in relation to painful human experiences, yet there is blessing hidden within them providing inherit ennobling and exalting power.

Jesus Christ is our Lord and Savior. Yet, on the cross under the weight of unimaginable pain and stress, His challenge was likely increased as recorded in Matthew 27:46.

> *And about the ninth hour Jesus cried with a loud voice, saying, Eli, Eli, lama sabachthani? that is to say, My God, my God, why hast thou forsaken me?*

Our Heavenly Father withdrew His Spirit, leaving Christ on His own to complete the most challenging, yet important trial necessary for the progression and sanctification of Father's children. The most exquisite resultant blessings available to us come about through Christ's completion of the Atonement in the Garden of Gethsemane and His crucifixion. Christ is perfect and yet was required to master the pain

He experienced and ultimately without the presence of Father. The challenge was not a punishment, but was essential for Christ and all of Father's children who come to earth.

Why was the earth's Creator and our Redeemer required to complete this act "totally alone"? I do not know why, but it is enough for me to know that He did it and Christ's example has infused additional love and light into this soul of mine. I have no anger in or about the challenges of my life when I turn to Christ with full purpose of heart, considering what He sacrificed for us, the pain he bore that could not be shared.

Peter, chosen by Christ to be the chief apostle, had experiences that tested his mind and heart together. Think of the test of Peter's faith and honesty when he denied three times knowing Christ at the trial held at the high priest's castle following the experiences in Gethsemane. What depth of guilt and pain do you think he felt?

Paul, an apostle and convert to Christ experienced much, both positive and negative. He participated in the stoning/martyrdom of Stephen who was an active follower of Christ. On his way to Damascus to continue the persecution of converts to Jesus Christ, he received a vision of the Savior and Paul's life was changed from that moment on. Can you imagine the pain he must have felt having been a persecutor of those early converts and discovering that all his effort, the anger and self-righteousness that must have filled his heart was all in error; an error that caused him to participate in the martyrdom of a faithful son of God, responsibility in taking the life of another. What kind of feelings and experiences do you think must have filled his quiet moments and days as he sought to repent from egregious sin?

Joseph Smith is the prophet who Christ called to restore His church after it was taken from the earth due to the death of the original apostles and the apostasy or the forsaking of true principles that followed after their deaths. Joseph was guided by the Savior and embraced the call to be the prophet of the restoration of Godly authority and the gospel upon the earth. His preparation began in his youth; difficult and painful experiences mixed with the profound and joyful. As is the pattern of preparation and progression with those whom God calls for significant service, Joseph suffered much. Joy, it seems, is often counterbalanced or tempered by pain. He was persecuted all of his life from age 14 until he was martyred 24 years later.

Perhaps you have witnessed as I have that this pattern is also the design for all of Father's family, preparing each of us for the present and future to be trustworthy children. Awakening, progression, failure, pain, repentance, conversion, joy, patience, faith, trust, love, they all seem to be necessary components in discipleship. Receiving and embracing truths refines and blesses our lives, but does not prevent us from experiencing pain. To have pain, to struggle, to be challenged is not a punishment, but a refiner of personal attributes and abilities as we must be tempered and schooled in order to align our lives with Christ on the sacred path of discipleship. Remember, discipleship requires us to follow Christ's example and to be a blessing in the lives of others as we serve them.

CHAPTER 27

⟐⟐⟐

JESUS CHRIST, THE SAVIOR

For behold, and lo, he shall come, as it is written in the book of the prophets, to take away the sins of the world, and to bring salvation unto the heathen nations, to gather together those who are lost, who are of the sheepfold of Israel;

. . . to prepare the way, and make possible the preaching of the gospel unto the Gentiles;

And to be a light unto all who sit in darkness, unto the uttermost parts of the earth; to bring to pass the resurrection from the dead, and to ascend up on high, to dwell on the right hand of the Father (JST, Luke 3:5-7, Joseph Smith's translation).

Here is a prophecy of the coming of the Savior and the work that He would accomplish while here in mortality. These are words of solace that should have lifted the spirits of those who heard them and brought joy and hope for the future, for the completion of the Lord's work to bring the fulfillment of salvation unto all who turned to Christ.

And the angel said unto them, Fear not: for, behold, I bring you good tidings of great joy, which shall be to all people.

197

For unto you is born this day in the city of David, a Saviour,
which is Christ the Lord (Luke 2:10-11).

Can you imagine being in that small gathering of shepherds and hearing the angel speak these words that should fill our souls with joy and thanksgiving each time we read them? To be a witness of the fulfillment of prophecy, to receive an invitation to see with your own eyes Father's blessing for all His children was an honor beyond description. Yet, that same spirit which the shepherds received, and which must have filled their hearts is available to us as we worship and give thanks for this Blessing of all blessings.

And suddenly there was with the angel a multitude of the
heavenly host praising God, and saying,
Glory to God in the highest, and on earth peace, good will
toward men (Luke 2:13-14).

Now, over 2,000 years since this hallowed event occurred and as we ponder, is it possible that you were among that *multitude of the heavenly host praising God.* Did we wait with anticipation for our turn to come to earth, knowing that Christ would perform the Atonement and that His church would be restored for us to receive the saving ordinances needed to return Home? Were our hearts filled with immeasurable joy? If only we could remember. However, Father in His love and kindness has given us the Holy Ghost who can witness with clarity the reality of these events and the eternal blessings that await the faithful.

Living to the Fullest

Perhaps you have heard this description before, when someone was trying in a few words to describe the way a person lived his life. "His life was lived to the fullest." I presume that this description could be interpreted in many ways, but most often I suppose people are trying to describe the person as living a life seen as complete, or one that always seemed jam-packed with variety and activities that appear fun, or rewarding, or fulfilling, or hard to duplicate.

There are endless examples both near and far of people living lives that we might wish for ourselves or at least some portion of them. Why? There are many reasons, but perhaps by being enamored with that which appears varied, or exciting, or romantic, or exotic, or physical, or mental, easy, or any of a hundred different experiences others have that tickle our imaginations; they may energize us to try and mirror their lives in some way. Are those examples of lives "lived to the fullest?"

Fullest suggests complete, lives that have all the elements that the Creator designed to prepare Father's children in order for them to return Home and become like Him. The other examples may seem desirable, but those factors by themselves are not sufficient to be complete. Understanding who we are and where we came from is a prerequisite for a life to be lived to the fullest. It can't be done without having a relationship with Jesus Christ, He who created the world for earthly and spiritual experiences to be had together.

We know that Father and Jesus Christ have physical bodies and are perfect or complete. Our lives, our beings cannot be complete without that which is spiritual, without the fulfilling growth and development of our "spiritual DNA," being refined and tested in the crucible of mortal experience.

Earthly experience was designed by our Father. Under His leadership, Jesus Christ is the Creator and the Redeemer, so that each of Father's children can and must make choices, experience outcomes, and prove to actively become disciples of Jesus Christ and align their lives with Father's will. All of this is being done for the day when they will have the opportunity to return Home, having proven themselves trustworthy regarding their responses to experiences in this temporal realm.

When we are baptized, we take upon us the name of Jesus Christ. Our prayers are to be offered in His name. The saving ordinances performed by priesthood authority in the temples and other sacred places are always done in the name of Jesus Christ. It is vital that we come to know Him and draw much nearer to Him, that is the design of mortality.

> *Behold, I am Jesus Christ the Son of God. I created the heavens and the earth, and all things that in them are. I was with the Father from the beginning. I am in the Father, and the Father in me; and in me hath the Father glorified his name.*
>
> *I came unto my own, and my own received me not. And the scriptures concerning my coming are fulfilled.*
>
> *And as many as have received me, to them have I given to become the sons of God; and even so will I to as many as shall believe on my name, for behold, by me redemption cometh, and in me is the law of Moses fulfilled.*
>
> *I am the light and the life of the world. I am Alpha and Omega, the beginning and the end* (3 Nephi 9:15-18).

Jesus Christ is the First Born, the Only Begotten of Father. He is the Savior, having met the requirements of eternal law in performing the Atonement that we all may have the opportunity of returning to Father's home if we follow Christ's instruction and example in our lives.

The Imagery of Relationships

Christ's description of Himself, our Father, those who are disciples, and our relationships with Him were given with powerful imagery that made it all very clear as He taught the apostles in the 15th chapter of John.

> *I am the true vine* (the true vine provides connection and nourishment to the branches and fruit), *and my Father is the husbandman* (the husbandman is the farmer, he who cultivates the land).
>
> *Every branch in me that beareth not fruit he taketh away: and every branch that beareth fruit, he purgeth it, that it may bring forth more fruit* (John 15:1-2).

It is vital to understand that bearing fruit or doing good is essential in this relationship, but it does not mean that the producing branches, which are Father's children, have arrived, so to speak, completing all that the Husbandman or Father requires of them.

Those children or branches that do not bear fruit are taken away and not permitted to be "joint heirs" with Christ. Those that produce are purged, meaning their refining and progression continues through life's challenges as impurities are refined from them. The notion that if we are faithful, life will get easier is not the reality.

> *And ye have forgotten the exhortation which speaketh unto you as unto children, My son, despise not thou the chastening of the Lord, nor faint when thou are rebuked of him:*
> *For whom the Lord loveth he chasteneth, and scourgeth every son whom he receiveth* (Hebrews 12:5-6).
> *Wherein ye greatly rejoice, though now for a season, if need be, ye are in heaviness through manifold temptations:*
> *That the trial of your faith, being much more precious than of gold that perisheth, though it be tried with fire, might be found unto praise and honour and glory at the appearing of Jesus Christ* (1 Peter 1:6-7).

As can be seen from these scriptures, the faithful are further purified so that they are capable of producing even more fruit. It may not be sufficient for us to say, "I am happy with what I can do," especially if with Heavenly Help we are capable of doing much more, if our weaknesses have been replaced by strengths. Christ's desire for all of us is to become like Him. Consider these two scriptures.

> *Be ye therefore perfect, even as your Father which is in heaven is perfect* (Matthew 5:48).
> *The Spirit itself beareth witness with our spirit that we are the children of God:*

And if children, then heirs; heirs of God, and joint-heirs with Christ; if so be that we suffer with him, that we may be also glorified together (Romans 8:16-17).

To suffer with Christ implies that we must meet life's challenges as He did in order for us to fulfill the mission we each have to complete in mortal life. The underlying message that comes from these scriptures is that we will receive instruction sufficient to align ourselves with Christ, if we desire it, and this will guide us to become complete or fully developed children of our Heavenly Father. We can count on having additional difficult challenges, which we must meet using Christ as our example, and with them there will be accompanying blessings that together mold us into who we are to become.

It likely will not be in Father's plan for us to rest at a comfortable place on the covenant path without progressing further. That thought is inconsistent with the spirit, requirements, and power of redemption. What makes sense is that with additional refining experiences we can become more like the Savior. This is in keeping with all that has been revealed about our temporal existence. Doing good doesn't mean we get to rest. Doing good qualifies us to do additional good as we continue developing, being refined by life's experiences and the Spirit, being worthy to receive the peace and joy promised to all faithful children.

Peace I leave with you, my peace I give unto you: not as the world giveth, give I unto you. Let not your heart be troubled, neither let it be afraid (John 14:27).

Returning to John, chapter 15, Jesus clarifies and expands His instruction.

Abide in me, and I in you. *As the branch cannot bear fruit of itself, except it abide in the vine; no more can ye, except ye abide in me.*

I am the vine, ye are the branches: **He that abideth in me, and I in him**, *the same bringeth forth much fruit: for without me ye can do nothing.*

If a man abide not in me, he is cast forth as a branch, and is withered; and men gather them, and cast them into the fire, and they are burned (John 15:4-6, emphasis added).

It is important to understand what the fruit is, so that we have a clear understanding of Jesus Christ, His mission, our relationship to Him, and expectations for us within that mission. Remember, the Lord has said that it is His work to bless Father's worthy children with Eternal Life. Knowing this, what is the fruit that the "branches" or Father's children are to bring forth? faithful and worthy daughters and sons. This is only possible if we "abide" in Christ.

To abide is to dwell or continue. Therefore, we dwell with Christ and He with us. This relationship is designed to "continue" without end. This can only happen if we accept Christ as the Redeemer, align our lives with Him, inviting and accepting His spirit to be with us, in other words becoming one with Him. To accept Christ means we will keep His commandments.

If ye keep my commandments, ye shall abide in my love, even as I have kept my Father's commandments, and abide in his love (John 15:10).

Christ is the vine and we are the branches, organized, integrated, and empowered with truth and light to bear fruit and for that fruit to remain, not to disappear, so that Father's gifts can be given and received, even the gift of Eternal Life.

Ye have not chosen me, but I have chosen you, and ordained you, that ye should go and bring forth fruit, and that your fruit should remain: that whatsoever ye shall ask of the Father in my name, he may give it you (John 15:16).

The bringing forth of fruit, providing sufficient support for it to remain, by asking for that which is needed from Father is not just the responsibility of those ordained to do so. It is the responsibility of all who are connected, who are aligned with Christ as branches of the "true vine" for the work of salvation and exaltation to take place.

> *And behold, I tell you these things that ye may learn wisdom;*
> *that ye may learn that when ye are in the service of your fellow*
> *beings ye are only in the service of your God* (Mosiah 2:17).

This instruction from King Benjamin to his people is as true and valuable today as it was in his day. It certainly makes sense as we focus on our relationship with Jesus Christ, the True Vine.

The way has been prepared from the organization of this world until this present time for all of Father's children to engage in the work of salvation, receiving that which is needful, not only for their own lives but to bless those who they serve. When we begin to comprehend that we are branches being connected to and nourished by the True Vine for the bringing forth of fruit, we come to understand there is much in responsibility and blessing that is intrinsic in this relationship.

Hopefully, when we engage in serving others, our hearts are filled with thanksgiving and we offer prayerful and humble appreciation to Father for our abilities and efforts. The giving of blessings to others is only possible because we are branches of the True Vine. Without this relationship any effort we might make would never be sufficient to contribute to the cause of salvation. The qualities we appreciate in others, including kindness, caring, love and thoughtfulness, are all present because of our connections to the True Vine.

If we honor this sacred link to the Savior and serve following His example and instruction, He identifies the outcomes that will bless our lives.

If ye abide in me, and my words abide in you, ye shall ask what ye will, and it shall be done unto you (John 15:7).

Ponder upon the trust and blessing this verse invites and promises for the faithful. It certainly implies that we will only ask for that which aligns with Christ's will. We have progressed sufficiently to understand and embrace who He is, who we are, what is important in life and how we can follow Him, serving and blessing others according to His example. In other words, we have become loyal and trustworthy. We are true disciples.

The Lord continued revealing the outcomes and attendant blessings of becoming a disciple.

Herein is my Father glorified, that ye bear much fruit; so shall ye be my disciples.

As the Father hath loved me, so have I loved you: continue ye in my love. (John 15:8-9).

How important it is to our salvation and exaltation to remember what it is to abide in the Savior's love; to accept Christ as our Redeemer and align our lives with His will. To abide in His love is to abide in Father's love. That witness is designed to fill our souls, increase our joy, and energize our efforts to fulfill our life's mission, including the bearing of fruit.

Fruit

In the imagery of the "true vine and branches" the definition of fruit we have used is the conversion of Father's daughters and sons to the light and love of the Savior, becoming faithful children. Certainly, this is the fruit we all want to be worthy of and of bearing for the blessing of others during our mortal journey. Fruit has been used throughout the scriptures identifying individual components that are reflective of the total composition of conversion and the outcomes or behaviors of those who have become converted. Let's identify some of them.

205

- Fruit from trees, Genesis 1:11
- Fruit of the womb, Luke 1:42
- Fruit of the righteous, Proverbs 11:30
- Fruit of the lips, Isaiah 57:19, Hebrews 13:15
- Fruit of thoughts, Jeremiah 6:19
- Fruits meet for repentance, Matthew 3:8
- By their fruits shall the faithful and wicked be known, Matthew 7:15-20
- Fruit unto life eternal, John 4:36
- Multiply the fruits of righteousness, 2 Corinthians 9:9-10
- Fruit of the Spirit, Galatians 5:22
- Forbidden fruit, 2 Nephi 2:15
- Fruit meet for Father's kingdom, Luke 6:44, D&C 84:58

Fruit is an outcome. It may be seen in the operation of the different physical components of this temporal world, or unseen to the mortal eye, having place in the heart and mind of man as in thought, speech, the exercise of gifts such as faith, love, attitudes, desires, efforts, trust, and patience. Desires, thoughts, mental and physical efforts, including those of the heart, all have outcomes, good or bad, they are the fruits of those life components.

The **summation** of all the righteous fruits, all the outcomes or gifts given is witnessed here in this instruction from Nephi.

> *Wherefore, ye must press forward with a **steadfastness in Christ**, having a **perfect brightness of hope**, and a **love of God and of all men**. Wherefore, if ye shall press forward, **feasting upon the word of Christ, and endure to the end**, behold, thus saith the Father: **Ye shall have eternal life*** (2 Nephi 31:20, emphasis added).

A love of *all men*—if we truly love God, we will have a love for *all men*. A person might mentally skip on beyond this statement, when reading, not realizing the import of Nephi's witness that to truly love God a love for *all men* must be a part of it. This may very well be a litmus test as to how pure and inclusive our love for God is. If you are not familiar with the term "litmus test," it is a term used figuratively regarding "a single factor that establishes the true character of something" (Merriam-Webster Online Dictionary). Our love for God is not a **pure love** unless it includes a love for all men.

Agency and Its Responsibilities

We have been looking at the example of Peter and numerous scriptures with a focus on Mosiah 3:19 to provide education to assist us in following the counsel from King Benjamin. The specifics on *becometh as a child* have been reviewed to provide clarity on our mortal journey to prepare us to be worthy to return to Father and Christ, to be in Their presence. Jesus Christ is the perfect example of heeding and applying King Benjamin's instruction.

Agency is a core component in the plan of salvation. The Savior's sacrifice had to be freely given; it could not be forced upon Him. Isn't this exactly the situation for each of us today? We have the right to choose, even as Jesus Christ did. Becoming a disciple of Christ and aligning our lives with Father's will for us is left to our agency, our decision. Think about the revelation given in Moses 1:39.

> For behold this is my work and my glory—to bring to pass the immortality and eternal life of man.

How is this done? The Savior's Atonement and resurrection paid the required price for immortality to be a free gift. The price was also paid for the gift of Eternal Life. However, it is conditional upon the decisions each of God's children must make regarding repentance and being faithful after receiving the opportunity to come to know who they are, who Father and Jesus Christ are. The decisions to align our lives with Father's will and to be true disciples of Jesus Christ require all that we have to give spiritually, emotionally, and physically.

We don't have the same ability as the Savior. However, we are required to make our progressive way on the covenant path, all in the example of Jesus Christ. We must refuse that which is born of darkness and the spirit of this world. Embracing light through the Savior who is the source of all truth and light, and making our way, growing and learning step by step, experience by experience until we are worthy to return Home through the blessing of the Atonement are the requirements that we must meet.

> *Behold, verily, verily, I say unto you, I will declare unto you my doctrine.*
>
> *And this is my doctrine, and it is the doctrine which the Father hath given unto me; and I bear record of the Father, and the Father beareth record of me, and the Holy Ghost beareth record of the Father and me; and I bear record that the Father commandeth all men, everywhere, to repent and believe in me.*
>
> *And whoso believeth in me, and is baptized, the same shall be saved; and they are they who shall inherit the kingdom of God.*
>
> *And whoso believeth not in me, and is not baptized, shall be damned.*
>
> *Verily, verily, I say unto you, that this is my doctrine, and I bear record of it from the Father; and whoso believeth in me believeth in the Father also; and unto him will the Father bear record of me, for he will visit him with fire and with the Holy Ghost.*
>
> *And thus will the Father bear record of me, and the Holy Ghost will bear record unto him of the Father and me; for the Father, and I and the Holy Ghost are one.*
>
> *And again I say unto you, ye must repent, and become as a little child, and be baptized in my name, or ye can in nowise receive these things.*
>
> *And again I say unto you, ye must repent, and be baptized in my name, and become as a little child, or ye can in nowise inherit the kingdom of God* (3 Nephi 11: 31-38).

(This is Joseph Smith's and Sidney Rigdon's testimony of the Savior following a vision they received as recorded in the Doctrine And Covenants.)

And now, after the many testimonies which have been given of him, this is the testimony, last of all, which we give of him: That he lives!

For we saw him, even on the right hand of God; and we heard the voice bearing record that he is the Only Begotten of the Father—

That by him, and through him, and of him, the worlds are and were created, and the inhabitants thereof are begotten sons and daughters unto God (D&C 76:22-24).

If we follow the Savior as directed and trust Him to get us where we need and desire to be, making offerings of our faith, hope, and actions, what is promised us? The answer was given by vision to Joseph Smith and Oliver Cowdery as they worked on the translation of the Gospel of John in the Bible.

And this is the gospel, the glad tidings, which the voice out of the heavens bore record unto us—

That he came into the world, even Jesus, to be crucified for the world, and to bear the sins of the world, and to sanctify the world, and to cleanse it from all unrighteousness;

That through him all might be saved whom the Father had put into his power and made by him (D&C 76:40-42).

What do you love in life? Do you love anything more than you love Jesus Christ? If so, it is vital to know that we have all been called to turn from the things of the world to love and follow the Savior of All Mankind. The pathway is in front of us. We need not fear. All the support needed to follow the Savior and become one with Him has been given and is maintained by a loving Father through His Only Begotten

Son. Our decision to follow Him is what is needed to invite receipt of all the blessings illuminated by the scriptures.

Perfected in Christ

Following the Savior, truly following Him requires so much more than a casual relationship. Consider this focused instruction from the Apostle Paul to Jewish members of the Church encouraging them to continue following Jesus Christ.

> *And ye have forgotten the exhortation which speaketh unto you as unto children. My son, despise not thou the chastening of the Lord, nor faint when thou are rebuked of him:*
>
> *If ye endure chastening, God dealeth with you as with sons; for what son is he whom the father chasteneth not . . .*
>
> *Furthermore we have had fathers of our flesh which corrected us, and we gave them reverence: shall we not much rather be in subjection unto the Father of spirits, and live* (Hebrews 12:5, 7, 9)?

Paul has condensed our relationship here with earthly parents and compared it to being obedient to our Heavenly Father. The need for instruction in order to make the most of our lives temporally and spiritually is identified here. This is the natural course of our lives, if we have received instruction with an obedient attitude, correction from both our earthly father and our Heavenly Father.

With this as background, how should we respond to the instruction from Christ that clearly says *Be ye therefore perfect.* Is perfection even possible for us in this fallen world? The Savior was the only perfect child of Father here in mortality. So, the answer is no, not here. But that doesn't mean that we cannot ever become perfect or complete as the scriptures instruct. If we are on the covenant path striving to be faithful, we can through Jesus Christ's power and the blessings of the Atonement become a "complete" person in the image of our Heavenly Parents. Here is the process.

And if men come unto me I will show unto them their weakness. I give unto men weakness that they may be humble; and my grace is sufficient for all men that humble themselves before me; for if they humble themselves before me, and have faith in me, then will I make weak things become strong unto them (Ether 12:27).

The design of mortal existence did not include Father's children coming to earth already complete. Nor would mortal existence, even with consistent striving, bring about perfection. This is not part of the plan. This doesn't excuse us from being determined to follow the Savior's example and spending a lifetime improving and progressing. It becomes obvious, as we ponder upon this scripture, that humility is one of the essential virtues that is needed for our progression. It is so important that weaknesses have been programed into the mortal journey to establish the necessary personal environment for humility to develop and thrive. Humility is a Christlike virtue.

Humility prepares us for this additional instruction from Moroni, which we examined earlier.

*Yea, come unto Christ, and be perfected in him, and deny yourselves of all ungodliness; and if ye shall deny yourselves of all ungodliness, and love God with all your might, mind and strength, then is his **grace** sufficient for you, that by his **grace** ye may be perfect in Christ; and if by the **grace of God** ye are perfect in Christ, ye can in nowise deny the power of God.*

*And again, if ye by the **grace of God** are perfect in Christ, and deny not his power, then are ye sanctified in Christ by the **grace of God,** through the shedding of the blood of Christ, which is in the covenant of the Father unto the remission of your sins, that ye become holy, without spot* (Moroni 10:32-33, emphasis added).

To fully appreciate the doctrine in this scripture, we must understand what grace is. Simply stated, grace is an attribute of God. It is an attribute of perfection that in its fullness contains all of the characteristics or qualities of Godly perfection, such as love, mercy and others. It is through grace that power is given to men to receive Godly attributes and to use them to assist God with His work. It is through grace that we are blessed with immortality and all the blessings available through the Atonement, including Eternal Life.

It should be obvious that these gifts of grace come to each person one at a time, not all at once. We must be worthy to receive them. We must deny ourselves *of all ungodliness.* Loving God with all our *might, mind, and strength* is essential.

Perfection in Christ is given to each soul, according to our development through Christ's grace. It is important to understand that we cannot become perfect or complete on our own. We therefore become perfect in Him through His grace as we continue striving on the covenant path. It is by grace that we are sanctified, having been forgiven of our sins, the price paid for them in the Atonement. As we progress in this manner, we will see and recognize the Lord's power sufficiently that it will be impossible to deny it. The refining of our souls will continue unto sanctification and ultimately become complete.

Divine Artistry

If you were painting a self-portrait, consider all of the steps that would be involved until it is complete. Do you think you might change the pose, maybe several times? What about the colors used? Do you surmise that you might make some mistakes or have changes of mind that will require repainting until it meets your standard for completion? What will happen if you invite others to give you critiques as you go along? Do you think this might inspire you to make some additional changes? This may be especially difficult if painting portraits is not one of your gifts, yet you won't be satisfied until it is done.

This might be a simplistic way to look at personal progression and finally becoming complete or perfect. Yet the steps involved and the possibility of making mistakes by following your own thoughts and expectations, misguidance from others, and having to learn and make changes as you go along, ultimately finding fulfillment and even joy in the process is not only a possibility, but is the expected outcome.

God is the ultimate artist and following His instruction is the only way the portrait will be completed, evidencing the beauty of every child. The steps will not be easy. Satan will try to convince us that we can paint by number—a method so much easier than Father's and totally unreliable, designed for corruption.

In the Lord's plan every portrait is unique, styled and colored with lines and hues that are from a divine palette, illuminating the uniqueness of each individual, yet with familiarity that testifies of the divine relationship between the Painter and the subject. The portraits do not have the sameness that Satan wants all of Father's children's portraits to have.

The only way the beauty of the soul can be discovered and captured in a life revealing portrait is through divine artistry. We can begin to see people as the Lord sees them by receiving a divine lens that is given to those who desire it by the Spirit. Seeing others in this way permits us to look beyond the mortal challenges, failures, and disfigurements and to see people as they truly are.

Consider Christ's passage through Jericho, and the throngs of people who wanted to see Him. Among those was a man named Zacchaeus and he was a publican, a tax collector, in fact he was chief among them. Zacchaeus wanted to see Jesus, but being short in stature, he could not see over the heads of those who lined the way. So, determined and not willing to be easily put off, he ran to a sycamore tree and climbed it to see the Savior.

When Jesus came nearby, He looked up and saw Zacchaeus among the branches and said to him, *Zacchaeus, make haste, and come down; for to day I must abide at thy house.* Witnessing this interchange, the crowd began to murmur that the Christ was going to be a guest of a sinner. Didn't he know that? And the scripture says that Zacchaeus *made haste, and came down, and received him joyfully* (Luke 19:5-6). *And Jesus said unto him, This day is salvation come to this house, forsomuch as he also is a son of Abraham.* **For the Son of man is come to seek and to save that which was lost** (Luke 19:9-10, emphasis added).

Christ saw through all the earthly circumstances and adornments that hid Zacchaeus' spirit from others and the Savior blessed him, seeing him for who he truly is. Aren't we all fellow citizens with Zacchaeus, sometimes being hidden from others by mortal garnishments, needing Christ's blessing? The promise is sure. He will see us for who we are. Will we follow Him?

At the End of the Day

In the city of Zarahemla, Alma began a mission throughout all the land to preach the gospel and to provide the instruction needed for his people to repent of their sins and put their lives in order. He began his instruction with this background regarding his father's labors to teach the gospel in this same land. He was called Alma after his father and is known in scripture as Alma the younger.

> *And behold, he* (Alma's father) *preached the word unto your fathers, and a mighty change was also wrought in their hearts, and they humbled themselves and put their trust in the true and living God. And behold, they were faithful until the end; therefore they were saved* (Alma 5:13)

Then, Alma the Younger asked his listeners a number of questions that are important for us to consider as we make our way on this mortal journey and certainly before "the end of the day."

> *And now behold, I ask of you, my brethren of the church, have ye spiritually been born of God? Have ye received his image in your countenances? Have ye experienced this mighty change in your hearts?*

Do ye exercise faith in the redemption of him who created you? Do you look forward with an eye of faith and view this mortal body raised in immortality, and this corruption raised in incorruption, to stand before God to be judged according to the deeds which have been done in the mortal body?

I say unto you, can you imagine to yourselves that ye hear the voice of the Lord, saying unto you, in that day: Come unto me ye blessed, for behold, your works have been the works of righteousness upon the face of the earth (Alma 5:14-16).

Have You Been Spiritually Born of God?

Nicodemus, who was a Pharisee and a ruler of the Jews, came to visit Christ one night, apparently hoping that he could come and go, not being seen by others. Obviously, he was intrigued by Christ, but his social and religious standing was at risk if he was recognized visiting with the "opposition" as judged by the Pharisees.

. . . Rabbi, we know that thou art a teacher come from God: for no man can do these miracles that thou doest, except God be with him (John 3:2).

Nicodemus appears to be genuine in his desire to understand Christ and His power to work miracles.

Jesus answered and said unto him, Verily, verily, I say unto thee, Except a man be born again, he cannot see the kingdom of God.

Nicodemus saith unto him, How can a man be born when he is old? can he enter the second time into his mother's womb, and be born?

Jesus answered, Verily, verily, I say unto thee, Except a man be born of water and of the Spirit, he cannot enter into the kingdom of God.

That which is born of the flesh is flesh; and that which is born of the Spirit is spirit (John 3:3-6).

Nicodemus's answer seems a bit facetious, but giving him benefit for trying to understand, it was important that he comprehend that Christ was speaking about being born spiritually. Christ explained to him that preceding being born of the Spirit, one must be born of water. Being born of water and the Spirit are required in order to enter into the kingdom of God. Father's children had been and continue to be born of the flesh. Now, it is vital for them to be born of the Spirit or of the Holy Ghost. This is to be a separate "birth" experience.

In the "new world," Alma the younger, following his experience with the angel (Mosiah 27:10-23) and the two-day period when he could not speak and had no strength in his limbs, he gained strength and spoke to the people that had gathered around him.

> *For, said he, I have repented of my sins, and have been redeemed of the Lord; and behold **I am born of the Spirit.***
>
> *And the Lord said unto me: Marvel not that all mankind, yea, men and women, all nations, kindreds, tongues and people,* **must be born again;** *yea,* **born of God,** *changed from their carnal and fallen state, to a state of righteousness, being redeemed of God, becoming his sons and daughters;*
>
> *And thus they become new creatures; and unless they do this they can in nowise inherit the kingdom of God* (Mosiah 27:24-26, emphasis added).

We were born of earthly parents, receiving a physical body, but in a fallen world. Now we must be born again, becoming children of God, so that we can become *new creatures*, and worthy to *inherit the kingdom of God*. The process or the ordinances that are needed, following repentance and faith in Jesus Christ, are baptism and receipt of the Holy Ghost. We maintain that worthiness by becoming true disciples of Jesus Christ.

Have You Received His Image in Your Countenance?

In receiving these sacred ordinances and becoming disciples of Christ, we also receive His Spirit to be with us. The sacramental prayers make this blessing very plain to our understanding.

> *O God, the Eternal Father, we ask thee in the name of thy Son, Jesus Christ, to bless and sanctify this bread to the souls of all those who partake of it, that they may eat in remembrance of the body of thy Son, and witness unto thee, O God, the Eternal Father, that they are willing to take upon them the name of thy Son, and always remember him and keep his commandments which he has given them; that they may always have his Spirit to be with them. Amen.*

> *O God, the Eternal Father, we ask thee in the name of thy Son, Jesus Christ, to bless and sanctify this wine* (water) *to the souls of all those who drink of it, that they may do it in remembrance of the blood of thy Son, which was shed for them; that they may witness unto thee, O God, the Eternal Father, that they do always remember him,* **that they may have his Spirit to be with them,** *Amen* (Moroni 4:3, 5:2, D&C 20:77, 79, emphasis added).

Having the Spirit with us, not only changes and fortifies us internally or in our hearts, but it also is visible in our countenances. Jesus Christ is the perfect example in this as in all things.

> *. . . and his countenance did smile upon them, and the light of his countenance did shine upon them, and behold they were as white as the countenance and also the garments of Jesus* (3 Nephi 19:25).

. . . God ministered unto him by an holy angel, whose countenance was as lightning, and whose garments were pure and white above all other whiteness (D&C 20:6).

Following the completion of the Sabbath and the Savior's resurrection, Mary Magdalene and the other Mary went to the sepulcher where Christ's body was laid. An angel from heaven came and rolled back the stone and sat upon it.

His countenance was like lightning, and his raiment white as snow (Matthew 28:3).

As recorded in the scriptures, the countenances of those who are filled with purity and the Spirit are difficult to describe, but nonetheless remarkable. Even on a lesser scale here in our everyday life, we can see the Savior's image on the faces and in the eyes of those who have the Spirit with them. It is likely that we are drawn to those whose countenances give us a visible witness of who they are and what fills them. The reverse is also true for those who align their lives with the adversary.

Have You Received this Mighty Change of Your Heart?

In a major address to all of his people, the Book of Mormon records that King Benjamin wanted to know if they believed in the words which he had spoken to them. He sent an inquiry among them to understand their responses and this is the reply he received.

*And they all cried with one voice, saying: Yea, we believe all the words which thou hast spoken unto us; and also, we know of their surety and truth, because of the Spirit of the Lord Omnipotent, which has **wrought a mighty change in us, or in our hearts, that we have no more disposition to do evil, but to do good continually*** (Mosiah 5:2, emphasis added).

What a glorious experience that must have been and so overpowering in its very nature for all to have come to know the truth through the Spirit. To have become one in purpose through the changes in their hearts is an outcome that is desirable for our families and other associations that are dear to us. Through the genuine exercise of faith in Christ, the blessings of truth will so align our thinking and desires, that we have no disposition to do evil and want to bless the lives of others, even being saviors (D&C 103:9), as needed.

The Spirit prompts repentance and baptism for all, for those who sincerely seek a relationship that will bless their lives and bring them closer to Jesus Christ. Can you imagine what it would be like to feel the power of loving Christ being exercised every day by all people in their relationships with each other, lifting their thoughts and desires to truth and light, to the Heavens, for the blessing of all? I am certain that this love has filled the souls of many in this day.

This mighty change would precipitate all of these focused actions, but maintaining them becomes the next step in our walk on the covenant path. All the guidance that we are given today from God's anointed leaders of the Church needs to be followed with humility and meekness. This is instruction for our world and has the points of doctrine that each of us needs to embrace to turn us from the spirit of the world to building the relationships we need with Father, Christ, and the Holy Ghost. This is for our maintenance; to protect us from the sin, depravity, and corruption the adversary has in place to fool and enslave us.

We have access to truth, light, the Spirit, and all the blessings that Father wants for His children, if we genuinely seek them and align our lives with His will. We must make decisions daily, even hourly, that keep our hearts focused on righteousness and our minds filled with obedient determination.

With a mighty change in our hearts, we will begin to trust God to get us where we need to be. We will be guided to do the sweet and simple things that will bless family and friends, as well as the greater efforts needed from time to time to keep us all connected, thriving, and fulfilling the stewardships and missions given from the Lord.

Sin would become an outlier, never embraced and would only be found occasionally and at great distance from the desires, efforts, and actions of Father's children from day-to-day as they diligently seek to live righteous lives. Perfection will still elude us, but we will learn from our mistakes and misjudgments, virtuous changes taking their place. Selfishness, pride, and other corruptive attitudes will be stripped away and banished from individual lives, having no room or desire for them in their souls.

A mighty change of heart embraces all that is needed for a righteous life.

Christ Is Our Advocate

My little children, these things write I unto you, that ye sin not. But if any man sin and repent, we have an advocate with the Father, Jesus Christ the righteous (JST 1 John 2:1, Joseph Smith's translation).

An advocate is someone who pleads our case to a person or organization which has authority to give or deny something we desire to possess or belong to. In the instruction from this scripture, John explains that Christ advocates our cause to our Father.

To gain a better understanding, let's look at a simple example in our culture. Have you ever been asked to believe in or support someone who needs assistance in proving their status and needing another person who can fill that need? Perhaps you have needed that kind of help to gain something that you could not get on your own?

Credit worthiness is a common requirement for purchasing something when we do not have the ability to pay for it outright. We end up needing a loan. If we don't have sufficient positive credit background and resources, such as a young person might need who wants to buy a car, but must obtain a loan for the purchase, then an advocate who might be better known as a parent may be needed.

The parent signs on the loan documents along with the child, essentially guaranteeing that the loan requirements will be met, even if the child is unable to meet them on his own. The parent is acting as an advocate, pleading the child's cause by guaranteeing the funds will be repaid, even if the parent must use her/his own resources to do so. Many of us have been that "child" at one time or another.

Christ in performing the Atonement acts as an advocate for all of us. He pleads our case to Father by using his unlimited perfection, wrapping it around our limited imperfections, to provide the cleansing and strengthening that is needed in our lives in order to be worthy to return Home and be in Their presence. The Apostle Paul bore this testimony.

> *For this ye know, that no . . . unclean person . . . hath any inheritance in the kingdom of Christ and of God* (Ephesians 5:5).

Christ instructed,

> *And no unclean thing can enter into his* (Father's) *kingdom; therefore nothing entereth into his rest save it be those who have washed their garments in my blood, because of their faith, and the repentance of all their sins, and their faithfulness unto the end* (3 Nephi 27:19).

We become perfect in Christ through the exercise of our faith, repentance, and baptism into His Church. Then, as we continue to progress on the covenant path, embracing all the saving ordinances, using Christ's infinite resources to get where we need to go, we will one day be worthy of obtaining perfection if we continue in faithfulness *unto the end.*

In the example of the child and parent working out the purchase of an automobile, the parent uses his resources, if needed, to bring about the desired result. Unlike Christ, the father may require the child to pay back any money he must pay on the loan.

The Savior's resources were used to pay "up front" for all of Father's children, the suffering of sins for all, even all those that had not even been born at that time. Not one of us will get through mortality without sin as Christ did. Christ's performance of the Atonement provided Him the power and authority to act as an intercessor or advocate to make an appeal to Father on behalf of those who accept Him and repent of their sins.

The price Christ paid is incomprehensible, for He made payment in full for all of our individual iniquities. Adam's fall introduced death and sin into mortality. No matter what we have done in life, death has been overcome and we will live on.

Where we will be following the Judgement and what we will enjoy and experience has yet to be revealed. To accept Christ as our advocate requires us to love Him, desiring to become "one" with Him, joining His unlimited resources with our limitations for our eternal benefit. We take upon us His name by baptism, striving to be faithful, to be good people, knowing that we cannot ever return to Father and Home without Him. In this way we become partners in our progression, or perhaps with greater emphasis, He becomes a Father to us.

Christ overcame death and the estrangement of man from God, because of sin. We cannot repay these two debts as they are gifts. However, instead of repayment, Father's desire for us is to be awakened to truth, filled with light, and progress according to the plan of salvation that was revealed to us when we were present in His Heavenly Home. That plan is being taught once again here in mortality, administered by Christ and those He has called to be His witnesses, apostles and prophets.

Conversion and progression on the covenant path are the requirements for us to be worthy to join Him in that Heavenly Home. Instead of repayment, Father's plan is for us to become complete (perfect) and faithful children through the Savior's perfection, and in so doing we verify that Christ's pain, suffering, and the gift of all that he had, using the power of Godhood, was not spent in vain.

Our blessing unto faithful progression and worthiness to be in Father's presence is the goal, the desired summation of all of Father's and Christ's efforts to bless His family. Even as earthly parents rejoice in the companionship of family, this joy is also one that will last forever, if we are near to Them.

Do You Exercise Faith in the Redemption of Him Who Created You?

Following the upheaval of the earth at the crucifixion of Christ, the tempests, fires and whirlwinds that changed the face of the Book of Mormon lands destroying cities, and brought the end of mortal life to many; the devastation leaving a powerful testimony of destruction and Godly power. The voice of Christ was heard describing what had taken place as He introduced Himself to those who still clung to life.

> *Behold, I am Jesus Christ the Son of God. I created the heavens and the earth, and all things that in them are. I was with the Father from the beginning. I am in the Father and the Father in me; and in me hath the Father glorified his name.*
>
> *I came unto my own, and my own received me not. And the scriptures concerning my coming are fulfilled.*
>
> *And as many as have received me, to them have I given to become the sons of God; and even so will I to as many as shall believe on my name, for behold, by me redemption cometh, and in me is the law of Moses fulfilled.*
>
> *I am the light and the life of the world. I am Alpha and Omega, the beginning and the end* (3 Nephi 9:15-18).

Christ made it clear that He is the Son of God, the Creator, and the Redeemer. He is the One who sacrificed His own blood to pay the price of sin for all of Father's children, providing the opportunity to receive all the blessings Father has for His children, if they would repent and turn to Christ.

> *Forasmuch as ye know that ye were not redeemed with corruptible things, . . .*
>
> *But with the precious blood of Christ, as of a lamb without blemish and without spot:*
>
> *Who verily was foreordained before the foundation of the world, but was manifest in these last times for you, . . .*
>
> *For Christ also hath once suffered for sins, the just for the unjust, that he might bring us to God, being put to death in the flesh, but quickened by the Spirit* (1 Peter 1:18-19, 3:18).

In Jesus Christ's own words and in the testimony of others, His preeminence pre-mortally and His sacrificial act in mortality as the Lamb of God were accomplished according to the will of His Father for the benefit of all.

Questions to Ponder

- Do you look forward with an eye of faith and view this mortal body raised to immortality, and this corruption raised to incorruption, to stand before God to be judged according to the deeds which have been done in the mortal body?
- Can you imagine to yourselves that you hear the voice of the Lord, saying unto you in that day: *Come unto me ye blessed, for behold, your works have been the works of righteousness upon the face of the earth* (Alma 5:16)?

CHAPTER 28

❖◦◦❖

A BRIGHT FUTURE

Loving Jesus Christ more than anything we have on earth is not a question that must be answered by only those that have leadership positions in the Kingdom of God. It is a question that must be answered by all of Father's children who have lived or who will live upon the earth. Our bright future, receipt of all of the blessings Father has available for His faithful children depends upon our love for Jesus Christ and our covenant to follow Him, to be a true disciple, to align our lives with His will.

What is required is a choice, one that we can't make casually. This choice requires us to come to know Jesus Christ by exercising and using the tools we have been given to do so. Think about those things you are passionate about, those things or activities that you zealously regard in life. Will they bring you closer to knowing Christ or will they encourage or assist you in wandering away? Our choice is the same as Peter's, (*Lovest thou me more than these?*)

What will our love for Christ require of us? Most of us will never know in advance what will transpire throughout our lives or how our steps in mortality will end. It appears that Peter had some knowledge of his end. Following the interview with Christ when he was called to feed the Savior's sheep, Peter's martyrdom was prophesied by the Savior.

*Verily, verily, I say unto thee, When thou wast young, thou girdedst thyself, and walkedst whither thou wouldest: but when thou shalt be old, thou shalt stretch forth thy hand, and another shall gird thee, and **carry thee whither thou wouldest not.***

This spake he, signifying by what death he should glorify God. And when he had spoken this, he saith unto him, Follow me (John 21:18-19, emphasis added).

*Knowing that shortly I must put off this my tabernacle, **even as our Lord Jesus Christ hath shewed me*** (2 Peter 1:14, emphasis added).

Peter knew his life would be taken. He also knew that he must fill his life with all that loving Jesus Christ required. He did so and history records his faithfulness, his loyalty, and his efforts to do all that the Savior required of him, blessing all of Father's children by bearing witness, instructing, leading, and sacrificing according to Christ's will. Through divine assistance, Peter's efforts, love, and devotion bear the same witness to us now as they did 2,000 years earlier. The underlying question for each of us is, are we willing to receive it?

With Peter's life as an example, what should our lives be filled with if we love Jesus Christ more than anything else in mortality? Shouldn't we bear witness of truth, instruct in Godly principles, give leadership where appropriate, and be willing to sacrifice anything that Christ requires of us to complete our life's mission? Faith will overcome all fear and love binds us together, all more powerfully than any effort by Satan to confuse, corrupt and destroy.

If ye love me, keep my commandments (John 14:15, emphasis added).

If ye keep my commandments, ye shall abide in my love (John 15:10, emphasis added).

How many times must Christ ask us before we can truthfully say unto Him, *Lord, thou knowest all things; thou knowest that I love thee* (John 21:17).

AUTHOR'S NOTE, CONTINUED

⤙◦C⟆∽⟇◦⤚

We must be cognizant that we are composed of two different parts—a spirit, being spirit children of our Heavenly Father, and a physical body that clothes our spirit, a gift through the love of mortal parents that is composed of earth elements. Hunger is an alert that comes to both parts of our being, but is satisfied in different ways. Our bodies need nourishment from ingesting the foods Christ has blessed us with in the creation, providing nourishment for health and energy.

Our spirits need interaction with that which is of Father and Son, providing spiritual nourishment, even to the refining and purifying of our beings for the preparation needed to return Home and be in Their presence. The health requirements for both body and spirit are real and come together in the faithful soul to be one in fulfilling the focus of earthly experience.

Let's return to the story I shared at the opening of this discussion. I found beauty and similarity in the life sustaining efforts of a hummingbird. To quickly review, the bird was flying and hovering around a Japanese Maple tree outside the window of my home office, obviously looking for a source of nectar, for satisfaction of hunger and physical need. No matter how sincere this effort was, it would not be productive, unless it learned that this tree had nothing to offer that would fulfill and sustain life.

I couldn't help making what is a broad comparison between the bird and our lives, as we, having mortal bodies, are looking for sustenance every day. Like the bird, we have a pretty good idea of our physical needs, hunger combined with thirst, these two provide sufficient motivation to search out what we require, much of the time not having to travel very far to find a meal. Experience is a valuable teacher. Some of us may look like we have found way too many meals, but that is another discussion.

Another observation is important as we look quickly at our physical needs. Not all available foods have the same nutritional content, providing the complete nourishment needed. Those foods lacking in helpful nutrition may be very enticing in a number of ways, like the glazed doughnut that is always a temptation for me. However, consuming them likely inflicts less than positive impacts on our body's operations. These consequences may lead to physical impairments we may not even recognize, but left unattended, may incite longer-term health issues.

Let's leave the physical component of our beings and focus on the spiritual. We are spiritual beings, now clothed with physical bodies and have experiences that are new, yet integral to our spiritual development. We are a lot like the hummingbird, flying around, hovering over things that catch our attention or interest us; the whole time looking for things that are pleasing and fulfilling in some way.

Temptations exist, affecting both our physical and spiritual selves. Everything in life requires choosing and often we don't know what our choices will bring us. Spiritual need and hunger, if ignored or only given lip service, will have consequences that keep us from progressing to our potential, according to our Father's desire for us. This status, if unchanged, will likely prevent us from fulfilling the mission we were given pre-mortally to complete as a joint-heir with Christ here in mortality (Romans 8:16-17).

I don't know that the comparison with the hummingbird holds up here, but think about all the things that are a part of your life, things that you choose to do—entertainment, education, service, physical exercise, rest, sleep, eating, recreating, worship, reading, the choices are innumerable, and we spend all of our time and much of our resource doing what the hummingbird does to fill up a day. We fly all around, hovering at times for what interests us or is demanded of us, but the unasked question is always in front of us—will this choice be a blessing for me, both here in mortality and beyond?

The evidence is in. We grow best from challenges, even difficult challenges that test our capabilities, but in marshalling our physical and spiritual gifts and abilities, we have the blessed condition to learn from them. That education, when in place, often provides the needed foundation for the next challenge that arises. This growth cycle seems to have no end, unless we choose to quit. What a tragedy that would be for our walk on the path to Eternal Life, to end by our choice.

This cycle is certainly no secret. Opposition seems to be everywhere present. Opposition can be a positive influence, depending upon our response, providing growth and production that could not come about any other way. Let's divert from this focus on opposition that we likely would characterize as a negative influence in our lives.

Let's look at a simple example. We can stand up from a sitting position because the earth opposes that action, providing a firm foundation to stand upon. OK, that was a very simple example, but it works. Here is another one. Baseball is a grand game utilizing opposition. When a batter steps up to the plate and a pitch is thrown, the energy or opposition that surrounds the ball is reversed when the batter hits it, and a new scenario unfolds.

The Lord uses opposition (much to the consternation of the adversary) for the increase of our abilities and gifts, if we meet it with faith and determination, trusting God to make it a blessing.

This is the foundation that puts us in charge. This is how we gain strength and wisdom, creating a new situation of blessing rather than an outcome of corruption.

Satan and his followers seem to know when we have had a spiritual experience that has awakened us to a greater understanding of who we really are and where we came from, or when we are being challenged by one of our weaknesses. Adversarial attempts at distraction, shaming, promoting lies, or whatever might turn our attention from a spiritual focus, show up all too timely to attempt to turn us from the Light.

Satan is a master at corruption and destruction. He uses lures just as we might use them to trap unsuspecting insects or vermin that we want to get rid of. Don't let yourself get trapped like a moth in a flame. Keep in mind this instruction from Jesus Christ.

> *But the Comforter, which is the Holy Ghost, whom the Father will send in my name, he shall teach you all things, and bring all things to your remembrance, whatsoever I have said unto you* (John 14:26).

Now, on a slightly different focus. Perhaps you have noticed throughout the pages of this work that love is a key component to all that is a blessing in our lives. It is integral to life itself. Victor Hugo, three days before his death, penned these words, "To love is to act." We have certainly seen the truth of this summation in the life of Peter. We can see that in action by the aligning of his life with the mission Christ gave him after the crucifixion and resurrection. He was strengthened and more deeply committed by growing from the opposition thrown at him.

At any time in our progress is this life, asking ourselves the questions that Alma asked his brethren will help us to more closely comprehend our relationship with Jesus Christ and make adjustments to answer "yes" throughout our lives.

> *Have ye spiritually been born of God? Have ye received his image in your countenances? Have ye experienced this mighty change in your hearts* (Alma 5:14)?

Is your heart filled with love? Do you love Christ more than anything else in your life? If so, has this love caused you to act in the ways of a true disciple? "To love is to act." *If ye keep my commandments, ye shall abide in my love* (John 15:10). Acting in the love of Christ will bring us to this essential question: *Lovest thou me more than these?* How will you answer? Remember, *For as he* (a person) *thinketh in his heart, so is he* (Proverbs 23:7).

BIBLIOGRAPHY

The Holy Bible, Salt Lake City, Utah, USA, The Church of Jesus Christ of Latter-day Saints, 2013, © By Intellectual Reserve, Inc.

Bible Dictionary, Salt Lake City, Utah, USA, The Church of Jesus Christ of Latter-day Saints, 2013, © By Intellectual Reserve, Inc.

The Book of Mormon, Salt Lake City, Utah, USA, The Church of Jesus Christ of Latter-day Saints, 2013, © By Intellectual Reserve, Inc.

The Doctrine And Covenants Of The Church of Jesus Christ of Latter-day Saints, Salt Lake City, Utah, USA, The Church of Jesus Christ of Latter-day Saints, 2013, © By Intellectual Reserve, Inc.

The Pearl Of Great Price, Salt Lake City, Utah, USA, The Church of Jesus Christ of Latter-day Saints, 2013, © By Intellectual Reserve, Inc.

OTHER BOOKS BY MICHAEL PURLES

———⊸∘⟨⟩∘⊶———

One-Day Miracles -Change Your Brain to Master
Your Weight
Turtletoes — Following the Steps of an Angel
Becometh as a Child
Embrace Ennobling Experiences

To know more about the author and his works,
please visit **michaelpurles.com**

ABOUT THE AUTHOR

———⊷◦⟡◦⊶———

Michael Steven Purles is an author who has served as a business skills trainer, as well as a business manager throughout much of his adult life. His writing opportunities have followed two parallel but different pathways, one for business and the other for personal life experiences. You will recognize in his writing a specific focus on finding strength for and helping to lift burdens that are a part of each person's life. A special focus is on our personal relationship with Jesus Christ and becoming one of His true disciples.

Michael and Jerry (his wife of 50+ years) have four children. Tracy, the oldest was born with congenital heart disease and lived to be 20. They have three sons, the second of which (according to birth order) also had congenital heart disease, but was able to be rescued by medical science. Michael's wife suffered a stroke three years ago and he graduated from being a husband only to a husband and caregiver.

You will find Michael's life experience filled with the joy of life and in relationships that go beyond mortality in his written works. You are invited to explore them.

www.ingramcontent.com/pod-product-compliance
Lightning Source LLC
Chambersburg PA
CBHW071722120626
46550CB00001B/346